The
Fabulous
Flathead

As told to

Sharon Bergman

by

J. F. McAlear

President of the Reservation Pioneers

Dedicated to the pioneers and others who
have made the Flathead Indian Reservation
the Fabulous Flathead that it is today.

 TREAS ST PUB CO , POLSON

THE FABULOUS FLATHEAD

PREFACE

Reservation Pioneers Inc. was organized at Polson on Aug. 16, 1959. Officers are D. A. Dellwo, Vice-president; Ruth Herreid, Secretary; Gladys Irish, Treasurer; George Piedalue, Ben Williamson, Helen Finley Stevens, J. S. Dillon, Frankie J. Proud, Directors; and myself, J. F. McAlear, President.

These are the same officers elected at the time of organization with the exception of Thomas Quinn, Director, who no longer lives on the reservation, and the late Lee T. Butcher, Secretary.

The primary purpose of our organization was to compile and perpetuate any and all historical data pertinent to the Flathead Indian Reservation.

This was a much larger task than anticipated but after almost three years of research and hard work, and with the cooperation of persons such as D. A Dellwo, Frankie J. Proud, Thain White, the Sam Johns papers, Hugh J. Biggar's thesis, and many other individuals, groups and publications — and especially our writer, Sharon Bergman — the book, "The Fabulous Flathead" is now complete and is hereby submitted for your approval.

J F. McAlear
President, The Reservation Pioneers, Inc,
Polson, Montana
July 23, 1962

The Fabulous Flathead

CHAPTER ONE
The Flathead Indian Reservation

Monumental decisions were made on July 16, 1855, at Council Grove, six miles west of present-day Missoula, which affected the lives and future generations of thousands of people.

An agreement was drawn up and signed by the United States government and three Indian tribes creating the Flathead Indian Reservation. Governor Isaac Stevens, representing the United States government, placed his signature on the document beside those of Chief Alexander of the Kalispel or Pend d'Oreille tribe, Chief Michelle of the Kootenai, and Chief Victor of the Salish Indians.

The outcome of the meeting found Chief Victor and his people remaining in the Bitter Root Valley, while the tribes of Chief Alexander and Chief Michelle were located in the newly-formed reservation in northwestern Montana.

"God's Country," as it was known to many, has a total area of 1,243,969 acres; it is eighty miles long at the extreme length and has an extreme width of forty miles. It is bordered on the east by the Mission Mountains, on the south by the Evaro Canyon and Squaw Range, on the west by the Cabinet Range, and the northern boundary cuts through the middle of the Flathead Lake.

Although Man created the Flathead Indian Reservation, the development of the country itself began millions of years ago with the uplifting of the mountains, and later by erosion as streams and glaciers filled the lower levels with soil. Then, it is believed, a great ice mass covered the region, filling the valleys with hundreds of feet of solid ice.

As warmer climatic conditions affected the area, freezing and thawing of the ice masses gave the region its present characteristics: rounded hills, pot holes, soil with high gravel content, and large boulders seemingly stranded at high elevations. With the final melting of the ice masses, a hill of five hundred feet elevation emerged at the southern end of the Flathead Lake.

When the lake began to overflow its natural boundaries, it drained through the Big Draw, west of Elmo, and rambled on westward through the Little Bitter Root basin. Later, the great force of this immense body of water created the present channel of the Pend d'Oreille River, now known as the Flathead River. This resulted in a much lower lake level, leaving the Big Draw country high and dry. The entire region was covered with good soil and eventually produced succulent bunch grass, a cattle man's paradise, both in the hills and valleys.

Prominent valleys on the reservation today include Valley View, Reservoir Valley, Moiese Valley, Irvine Flats, Round Butte, Mission Valley, Jocko Valley, the Big Draw, the Little Bitter Root, and Camas Prairie. The now larger Flathead River is snow-fed by the mountains that surround it. The Mission Mountains feed Mud, Spring, Crow, Post, and Mission Creeks, also the Jocko River on the south.

The altitudes on the reservation vary greatly. They range from a low of 2,530 feet above sea level west of Dixon to a high of 3,579 feet at the upper level of the Jocko Valley, southeast of Arlee. At Polson, the elevation near the river is 2,925 feet.

Extreme temperatures during the winter and summer vary immensely, from 104 degrees in the summer to 40 degrees below zero in the winter—but these extremes are quite unusual. The thermometer never reaches zero during some winters, and seldom hits 90 degrees during many summers. Other parts of Montana are frequently more extreme due to their geographical location; the reservation lies protected, west of the main range of the Rockies. The water of the Flathead Lake tempers the climate in the winter and cools the atmosphere somewhat in the summer. The average rainfall for the entire reservation yields about 15 inches of precipitation a year, with the greatest amount falling on the Mission Mountains, near Mission, and the least amount measured near Lone Pine and the western part of the area.

Before the advent of the explorer, the trader, and the settlers, the area was a haven for wild game. The lakes and streams were well-supplied with fish. It was a paradise for the early-day Indian as he never wanted for wild berries, meat, fish and timer for his home and fuel.

It was indeed a favored land, and today, although the supply of game and fish has been greatly depleted, the area still retains much of its natural beauty. It reflects the majestic power it once held when the valley was silent except for the footsteps of nature.

The Big Draw — Flathead Lake's first outlet

(Meiers Studio Photo)

Present outlet at Polson lowered lake level some 500 feet

(Meiers Studio Photo)

Water forced way through rock formation. This is Kerr damsite.

4

(Meiers Studio Photo)

CHAPTER TWO
Original Inhabitants

For many decades, anthropologists and historians have tried to wrest the early history of the Flathead country from artifacts, memories, and the ground itself.

Although many of the experts are not in complete agreement about the origin of the historic tribes that inhabited the area, specimens unearthed at various elevations on the hills around Flathead Lake indicate that several tribes occupied the region in earlier centuries. Very little is known about the inhabitants of this country before the arrival of the fur traders in 1807, but it is believed that during the 17th and 18th centuries, it was occupied by several small tribes of Indians: the Flathead, the Pend d'Oreille, the Kalispel, the Spokane, the Semte'use, and the Tuna'xe.

When the white man first explored the country, he found three major tribes: the Salish, commonly known as the Flatheads; the Kalispel, know as the Upper Pend d'Oreille; and the Kootenai.

It is believed by one authority, Dr. Turney-High, that the Salish Indians originally came from the upper Klamath region in Oregon and were descendants of the Semte'use Part of the tribe moved to Montana as a result of an argument in which they were the losers. The main tribe quarreled and fought over whether ducks quacked with their bills or their wings.

During the 1700's, according to J. A Teit, an anthropologist, the Salish tribe occupied the Deer Lodge valley, and the "Wide-head" of the Flathead people lived in the Jocko and Bitter Root valleys

The Salish migrated into the Flathead territory, and the tribes mingled and eventually cultivated both tribes into one, which is now know as the Salish. With the impact of the new culture, the Flatheads gradually eliminated the practice of flattening the skulls of their children.

When the Kalispel Indians arrived in the area (believed to have come from the Sand Point, Idaho, region), they found the Semte'use tribe already there. Known as the "Foolish Folk," the Semte'use were far from popular with other tribes, and both the Kalispel and the Salish Indians waged a war of extermination against them. The culture of the "Foolish Folk" is little known, but it is believed that they lived in holes in the ground, wore no clothes, and hunted and fished for their existence. They had arrow points made of a black stone, and metal beads of raw copper and zinc have been found and traced to them. Physically, they were very dark in color, short and powerful. Their narrow sloping heads were given credit for their foolishness. Their stupidity decimated them, for it is said that most of them perished, following their Chief over the Spokane Falls.

In the early 17th century, according to Dr. Turney-High, the Tuna'xe Indians left the area around McLeod, Alberta, and settled in the Kootenai River region in north Idaho and northwestern Montana. These people later became known as the Kootenai Indians. Their migration took them from Bonner's Ferry, Idaho, to Libby and Jennings, Montana, and thence on to Somers and the Elmo area around the Flathead Lake.

With the migration of the Salish, Kalispels, and the Kootenai, there was a filtering of culture between the Plains and Plateau through the Lower Flathead, and the local culture retained elements of both. Stone was used in making of arrows, spears, knives, pestles, hammers, and pipes. There was very little wood or bone work, but hair, bark and twine were used to make bags and other containers by all the tribes except the Salish. The Kalispel Indians were noted canoe experts in crossing the river at the foot of the lake, and their prowess was used on the lake and other streams.

Roots, berries and fish were the main foods of the Indians although the Salish tribe continued to hunt buffalo twice a year on the plains in the Blackfeet country around Browning and Cut Bank. Later all three tribes combined forces for protection and entered the Blackfeet area for their hunt. Although bloody encounters ensued with the natives east of the mountains, the three tribes held their own against the greater numbers of the Blackfeet because of their superior archery and bravery.

Family life with the early day Indians was fairly plain and simple. Monogamy was the custom although the only check on polygamy was economic. Children were well-cared for, but not spoiled.

The Indian Braves were responsible for the meat supply and hunted deer, elk, moose, mountain goats, sheep, gophers, muskrats, prairie chicken, grouse, ducks, geese, and fish. While the men hunted, the squaws gathered the important plant foods, which were the bitterroot, camas, wild onions, several kinds of berries, and the inner bark of the yellow pine. Unlike the Plains Indians, the Indians of the lower Flathead depended considerably on fish for the major part of their diet.

The hunting of big and small game was largely done individually, although some stalking was done in larger groups in the fall when the animals were in prime condition. The animals were dressed-out, with the meat being dried for consumption and the skins being tanned for use in making moccasins, robes, clothing, and tepee covers. The furs were used mainly for winter headgear or ceremonial garments.

Politically, each of the tribes had a hereditary head chief. The individual bands and villages into which each tribe was subdivided were ruled by a sub-chief. War chiefs, who were usually selected yearly and held this position as long as they were influentially great, led the war parties. A council of old men and the bravest warriors acted as advisors to the big chief.

Early settlers often commented on the two attributes for which the Indians of this region were noted—courtesy and relative virtuousness. Another quality of the natives was their apparent pacifism. Although the Salish and Kalispel had a few small wars among themselves or other tribes, especially the Blackfeet, the tribes were generally at peace with their neighbors. It has been noted that the three tribes never took the life of a white man in war.

In their religion, the Indian believed in a great variety of spirits, both good and bad. The medicine man was an important individual, and both men and women took their problems to him for guidance and counsel. The legends of these tribes abound in stories of giants and humanized animal characters, such as the "Coyote" or "Bear "

One of the legends tells of an Indian, Shining Shirt, who was a hero to both the Salish and the Kalispel. Shining Shirt predicted that men with fair skins and long black robes would one day come to teach the truth, to give new moral law, and to stop the wars with the Blackfeet. After the coming of the Black Robes, other fair skins would arrive and overrun the country. Shining Shirt, who used the sign of the cross, said the fair skins would make slaves of his people, but they should not be resisted

Lasso Stasso was a noted medicine man of the Kootenai tribe during the early 1900's. Born in Arlee, Montana, January 6, 1871, Lasso was the product of two tribes— three-quarter Kootenai and one-quarter Flathead. As a young boy of eleven years, he often hunted with his dog near what is now Finley Creek, near Arlee. On one such hunting trip, he saw a black bear swimming the stream. As Lasso put it, "Bear stopped, talked to me. Bear make me smart. He make me medicine man. Bear say, 'You sing to Indians; give them medicine for many purposes— for women having babies and for nearly everything else.' Bear give Lasso songs and power."

Soon after this experience, Lasso and his family moved to Dayton, near Flathead Lake. One night, at the top of Chief Rock above Black Lake, near Dayton, Lasso communed with the spirits.

"There Coyote spoke to Lasso. Coyote gave Lasso song. Deer gave Lasso power to hunt successfully. Fawn gave Lasso power to be shrewd gambler. Fawn also gave Lasso good love song."

After many love affairs, he finally married. His first wife gave him eleven children; his second wife bore him eight more. His reputation as a medicine man was good.

The ritual and songs that he used were simple but dramatic. His voice was deep when he sang, and his range of tone was very wide. In addition to his own songs, he used a nupeeka—a paraphernalia of a few strips of fur tied together with cord on which small bells were attached. Lasso would first pass the nupeeka over the sick person's chest, then down on the arm, then over the head, and subsequently over the rest of the body. He would generally be accompanied in song by his wife and another Indian woman, who would sing in softer voices. Even when an old man, his wisdom and treatments were sought by younger men and women from far and near.

His later days were spent in a type of melancholy as he longed for the return of the early days when his people had an abundance of game, meat, fish, and berries. He entered his Happy Hunting Ground from the Sisters' Hospital in St. Ignatius, December 23, 1951 at the age of eighty.

Many of his descendants are still living, including two of his daughters, Mary Stasso Antiste and Cecille Stasso Kallowat, who make their homes near Elmo and Dayton.

Chief Koostatah, noted descendant of Kootenais who came to Flathead in 1700s.

10   (Great Falls Tribune Photo)

CHAPTER THREE
Explorers — Furtraders

The forerunner of the development and exploration of the territory of Montana was the Lewis and Clark expedition.

Following the Louisiana Purchase of 1803, which included the territory of Montana, an impetus was given to explore the vast region between the Mississippi River and the Pacific Ocean. President Jefferson, in an endeavor to determine the most direct route across the continent to the west coast, appointed his private secretary, Meriwether Lewis, and William Clark to search out a route to the Pacific and to gather information about the Indians and the Far West.

Following a winter of extensive training, the 1st Regiment of the U S. Infantry, of which Lewis and Clark were captains, set out in 1804 from St Louis and began their journey up the Missouri. During the course of the expedition, Lewis and Clark discovered the source of the Missouri River, near Townsend, and were responsible for charting and naming three rivers — the Jefferson, the Madison, and the Gallatin

Their guide in crossing the Rockies was an Indian woman, Sacajawea, who aided them many times in their tortuous trip After wintering on the coast, they began their return journey, splitting up the party temporarily to follow separate routes along the Marias and the Yellowstone. Their journey ended in St Louis in 1806, and opened vast new territories to knowledge

Further exploration and the development of the territory of Montana was spearheaded by two fur companies, the Hudson Bay and the Northwest

David Thompson, the first white man to see the Flathead Indian country, was sent by his employers, the Northwest Fur Company, to explore the Montana territory in 1808, and to establish trade with the Indians. Leaving Winnipeg, he and his party followed the north fork of the Saskatchewan River in Canada, crossed the Rockies, then descended the west slope of the Kootenai River into Montana. The first trading post was established where the present-day town of Libby stands, with Finan McDonald and James McMillan left in charge to trade merchandise for furs.

The following year, the post was moved ten miles east, where the town of Jennings was eventually founded, but business did not warrant the continuance of the post and it was abandoned.

In 1811-12, David Thompson returned to the territory and built another trading post, the Saleesh House, near the present site of the town of Thompson Falls. From this headquarters he ranged far and wide, dealing with the Indians, trading beads, jewelry, tobacco, and other merchandise for pelts. Lone traders had dealt with the Indians, trading inferior goods; Thompson was the first trader representative of a known fur company in their midst and the Indians were friendly and cooperative due to his satisfactory bartering.

Thompson's fair dealing so impressed the Flathead Indians that they offered friendship as well as fur pelts. Making a trading trip to the main camp, near present-day Dixon, Thompson was told about the Flathead Lake and the surrounding country When he showed an interest in seeing the lake, the Indians provided a guide, and on March 1, 1812, David Thompson and his party topped a knoll — near what is now the McAlpin Ranch, five

What David Thompson saw — March 1, 1812

Looking eastward — Mission range

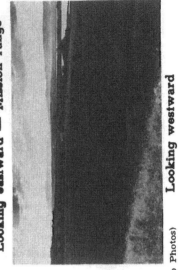

Looking westward

Looking northward — Flathead Lake

Looking southward

(Meiers Studio Photos)

13

miles northeast of Polson — and were the first white men to view the majestic beauty of the Flathead Lake. Greatly impressed, Thompson made extensive observations and surveys of the area before returning to the Dixon camp that evening.

Although David Thompson did not return to the Flathead Lake region, his trusted lieutenant, and an employee of the Northwest Fur Company, Jacques (Jocko) Finlay, went into the southern part of the reservation area at a later date and traded quite successfully with the Indians of the region

Jocko Finlay, born in 1768 in Montreal, was the son of James Finlay, Sr who married a Chippewa Indian woman A Frenchman, the elder Finlay was one of the founders of the Northwest Fur Company Working for his father's company in 1798, young Jocko distinguished himself as the defender of the fur company's post on Bow River in Canada Attacked by 150 hostile Indians, Jocko and three other men successfully held the post until help arrived.

In 1809, Jocko Finlay assisted David Thompson in building the Kalispel House on the Pend d'Oreille Lake. He was in charge of the Spokane House, another fur trading post, until May, 1828, at the time of his death

It is believed that the Jocko River and the Jocko Valley were named in honor of this popular fur trader, and many of his descendants now live on the reservation at the present time One of his grandsons, Piol Finley, was a very shrewd Indian who delighted in horse-trading with the "whites" in the Polson area around the turn of the twentieth century Finley Point was named for Piol Finley because of his residence in the area. Helen Finley Stephens, a director of the Reservation Pioneers, is a

14

daughter of Piol Finley, and she now resides near Arlee, Montana.

The Blackfeet tribe, occupying the upper reaches of the Missouri River, from Fort Benton west into the Montana territory, harrassed the fur trading industry for several years following the establishment of the trading posts. In an effort to combat the difficulties, the fur companies sent Iriquois and other eastern tribe Indians into the region to teach the friendly Montana Indians the ways and means of fur-trapping Their influence reached beyond fur-trapping Mingling with the Flathead (Salish) and the Pend d'Oreille Indians, they told stories about the white medicine men, The Black Robes, who could work Big Medicine Thinking the Black Robes could help them prevail over their enemies, the Blackfeet, the local Indians wanted a council with these white medicine men

In 1831, The American Fur Company arranged just such a meeting and transported four Indians, headed by Silver Eagle and Running Bear, to St Louis where they met with Captain William Clark, then Governor of the state of Missouri Having passed through their territory in 1805, Governor Clark was sympathetic with their desires, but he was unable to locate even one Black Robe or missionary willing to endure the hardships and danger of hostile Indians. Although better relations resulted at the outset of this historic meeting, the tribal ambassadors were unable to report to their people All four of them died before they could return to their tribes

There was eager competition for the fur trade in the great northwest during the 1830's, and into this picture enters the influence and impact of Angus McDonald

Angus was born at Resshire, Scotland, on October 15, 1816 After graduating from college, as a lawyer, Mc-

Fort Connah — first trading post
(Great Falls Tribune Photo)

Donald emigrated to America, and in 1838, entered the
employ of the Hudson Bay Fur Company. The following
year he was given the responsibility of being the chief
trader for the company in the Montana territory, covering the trading posts at Fort Hall and Fort Colville, and
also Fort Boise in Idaho.

The name of Angus McDonald was soon known far
and wide in the Indian territory; his reputation for being
fair in all dealings preceded him. The influence he had
with the Indians was reciprocated in more than one way
— he fell in love with a sister of Eagle of the Light, a Nez
Perce Chief. Beautiful Catherine and Angus were married
at Fort Colville in 1840. To this union were born thirteen
children; nine boys: John, Duncan, Archie, Thomas, Angus P., Donald, Joe, Angus C., and Alexander; and four
girls: Christine, Annie, Maggie, and one who died in in-
fancy.

In 1845, Frank McArthur established a trading post
at Fort Connah, which was approximately six miles north
of St. Ignatius. The next year the Hudson Bay Company
put Angus McDonald in charge of the fort to complete

16

the undertaking, and a total of eighteen buildings were finished in 1847. One of these buildings is still standing today — a memorial to the McDonalds and the fur trade.

In 1850, a big pow wow was held at the present site of Polson. Angus, stripped and painted with rich colors, rode his big black charger with skill. He matched the best of the natives in the competition, seemed to thoroughly enjoy himself, and won the admiration of all who competed with him.

Angus was in charge of the Fort Connah trading post for many years. His business thrived because of his fair dealings, and as just illustrated, his popularity with

Grandson Walter McDonald at Angus McDonald's grave

17

the Indians grew to such an extent that he was included in many tribal activities

In 1864, Angus was promoted by the fur company to general supervisor of the various trading posts in the region His son, Duncan, took over the reins at Fort Connah and guided the post successfully The earlier training that Duncan had received from his father in trading with the Indians held him in good stead

Gold was discovered in the territory in 1861. Francois Finlay took some panned mineral to McDonald, and explained that he had found it near Gold Creek in the Deer Lodge valley Angus sent the sample to headquarters at Fort Colville, and the report came back that it was almost pure gold Knowing full well that the discovery of gold would mean the end of the fur business, Angus grubstaked Finlay nevertheless Finlay didn't follow through, however, he panned a few ounces of rich ore, then quit the site

Ten years later, other miners were more persistent, and gold mining really opened up In 1871, the Fort Connah trading post, the last remaining one operating in the territory, was forced to close, and brought an end to a fabulous era

CHAPTER FOUR
Montana Missionaries
— Catholic Missionaries —

Ten years after the unsuccessful attempt by the Indians to bring the Black Robes to the Montana territory, another group of braves were sent to St. Louis and were successful in their efforts. They received a promise that missionaries would be sent the following year

In April, 1840, Father Pierre Jean DeSmet, a young Jesuit priest of Belgian birth, set out from St. Louis to fulfill this promise. Leaving Westport (now Kansas City) with a party of American Fur Company traders, he headed for the great northwest. On June 30, 1840, he was met at Green River, Wyoming, by a large band of Flathead braves who had been sent to meet this man of God They escorted him into the territory through what is now Monida Pass, and joined the main tribe of the Flathead, headed by Chief Big Face The tribe had been joined by members of the Nez Perce and Kalispel Indians, until they numbered about sixteen hundred

Christianity was first preached in Montana where the Beaverhead River empties into the Jefferson — where the town of Dillon stands today. Some two hundred Indian children and fifty adults were baptized. After two months of missionary work among the Indians, Father DeSmet returned to St. Louis, promising to bring other missionaries to the region next year

In the spring of 1841, Father DeSmet made good his promise Accompanied by two priests — Father Gregory Mangarini and Father Nicholas Point — and three laymen of the church — Joseph Specht, an Alsacian, and Charles Huet and William Claessens, both Belgians — he began the arduous journey Leaving Kansas City on May

10, 1841, they didn't reach their destination until August 30th. They were met by a group of Flathead braves, and after a few days rest, the party proceeded eastward through the Big Hole, crossing the Continental Divide at Deer Lodge Pass, descending into the Deer Lodge valley, and on toward Hell Gate Canyon.

By this time, the food supplies had dwindled, and the party was a large one. Although four two-wheel carts and one wagon were loaded with supplies for the new mission — axes, altar, supplies, blankets, books, and even an organ — supplies that would sustain man's soul, they had nothing to sustain man's body.

Stopping by the side of a river, they took stock of the situation. Some of the braves fashioned crude fishing gear, and were able to catch a large number of finny tribe, but not enough to supply the group until they reached their destination. Into this hopeless situation rode a small band of Flathead braves who were well-supplied with dried buffalo A feast, such as it was, was enjoyed by all before the party continued over mountainous country which had never carried a wagon wheel.

Father Mengarini wrote: "If the road to the infernal regions were as uninviting as that to its namesake (Hell's Gate) few would care to travel it."

The route was less than a trail, so steep that often the missionaries were required to attach ropes to different parts of the wagons to keep them upright At times they had to unhitch the Missouri mules, and pull the wagons by long ropes, easing their precious cargoes over ledges more suitable for mountain goat travel

When the party arrived at what is now Missoula, they camped for a few days while the missionaries decided on a permanent location for the mission.

On September 24, 1841, the first Catholic Mission in the territory was established twenty-eight miles south of Missoula, between what is now Stevensville and old Fort Owen A conspicuous cross was hewn by Father De-Smet, and placed in the center of a circle that had been cleared. Following a short service by Father DeSmet, all the Indians, young and old, came forward and solemnly kissed the cross and declared an oath that they would never forsake the religion of the Black Gown.

Following the dedication of the mission, the missionaries, their assistants, and some of the Indians set to work to erect a log church and a missionary's residence. The building consisted of log walls, with dirt floors and sod roofs. Deer skin was used for windows and partitions. On the first Sunday in October, 1841, the first church services were held

The next spring, wheat and potato seed were brought in from Fort Colville as well as milk cows. Fields which had been fenced were sown with the seed. Before Father DeSmet left the territory for work in Oregon and California, in 1845, a small grist mill, given to the Father in Antwerp, was installed, and a crude saw mill was constructed with wagon wheels and a saw.

Father Zerbinatti succeeded Father DeSmet at the mission, but his appointment was ill-fated. Father Zerbinatti drowned while swimming in the Bitter Root river.

Father Anthony Ravalli, an Italian, was sent to replace Father Zerbinatti, and a tribute to his work remains today. The town of Ravalli and Ravalli county were named for him, and the St. Mary's Mission church, which he helped build, is now the oldest existing church in Montana today. Father Ravalli had studied medicine, and he

21

was truly the Medicine Man to the Flatheads He performed many surgical operations and ministered vaccine and medical care when needed. Although he charged no fees for this service, he gratefully accepted gifts to the Mission from those who were able to contribute

By 1847-48, many of the older Indians had passed away, and the younger generation were not as devout in the new religion. They wished to return to the old way of life, and some of the white men coming into the region did all they could to help. Adding to the decline in attendance, the Mission was harrassed from time to time by marauding Blackfeet In 1850, the Fathers decided to close the Mission, and on November 5th, Major John Owen, an American fur trader, took possession of the property. Owen and his men, trained to defend themselves against hostile Indians, immediately built an adobe stronghold that became known as Fort Owen. Major John Owen eventually made friends with the Flatheads, and with one in particular — he married her

— The St. Ignatius Mission —

Father Adrian Hoecken, a Jesuit Priest, journeyed from St Louis and joined Father DeSmet in founding a mission on the Pend d'Oreille river It was near the Idaho-Washington line, in a beautiful valley headed by a waterfall which was nearly two hundred feet in height. The waterfall was used to power the mills. Father DeSmet's work took him to Walla Walla, and when he returned the next year he found that Father Hoecken had erected substantial buildings, grain had been sown, and the livestock acquired from St Mary's was flourishing. But the river, which was thought to be of such value, soon became a menace by late spring, flooding the crops and taking with it the seed and cultivated top soil

22

By 1854, the missionaries and loyal Indians, not to mention their livestock, were on the verge of starvation. At this point, a Kalispel Chief, who had received the name of Alexander at baptism, offered to show the Fathers another site beyond the mountains to the east He called it the Rendezvous — a place where bartering and gaming were indulged in by the tribes of the Kalispel, the Kootenai, Pend d' Oreille, and the Flathead It was in a valley between two mountains, not far from a great mass of water, and considered common ground by the adjacent tribes.

Swiss-born Father Joseph Menetrey and Brother Mc-Gean, an Irishman, accompanied Chief Alexander to the proposed location They found the Rendezvous to be a perfect site for the new mission — wonderful soil, good grasses, plenty of water furnished by creeks and springs, and timber nearby which could be used for council fires, logs, and lumber for building They made their report to Father Hoecken, and after much deliberation, the Jesuits decided to move. Father Hoecken sold the cattle for $2,600, mission possessions were packed, and the long trek to the east began

Father Hoecken and his party — Chief Alexander, Father Menetrey, and three lay brothers, McGean, Claessens, and Specht — arrived at the Rendezvous on September 24, 1854, which is the official date of the founding of the St Ignatius Mission in Montana. A log hut, which still stands, was erected for the missionaries. Tepees were set up, game was killed, and roots and berries were gathered as provisions for the winter Before the end of that fruitful year, eighty-two Indians had been baptized, a chapel. two houses, a carpenter and blacksmith shop were built, and word spread throughout the north that the Black Gowns had arrived at the Rendezvous.

By Easter, 1855, over one thousand Indians — Kootenai, Flathead, Kalispel, and Pend d' Oreille — had arrived to make their homes near the new Mission. By 1856, twelve log houses had been built, a flour mill was erected, and a saw mill begun. Barns were built to shelter livestock brought in from Fort Colville as sustenance for the missionaries and their helpers.

The missionaries worked closely with the Indian agent in an effort to improve the lives of the tribes. The government encouraged them to plant crops, furnished the seed, and the Indians took the harvest of wheat to the flour mills at the Agency or the Mission. They left a small share of the crop to pay for the milling, and received flour

Missionaries' first home at St. Ignatius

and feed for their livestock. The Indians bartered for lumber in the same manner, receiving finished lumber for the timber they took from their lands, and leaving a small share to pay for the milling.

Improvements continued at the Mission, and in 1864, the first nuns arrived in the Montana territory. Four Sisters of Providence came from Oregon to open a girls' school and a hospital. The girls were taught the rudiments of Home Economics — sewing, cooking, and housekeeping. The Jesuits opened a boys' school at the Mission, teaching such crafts as leather, iron and wood work. The leather craft work was the most popular with the Indian boys as it was associated with horses.

The first aid from the government was obtained in 1874, when the Mission was allotted $2,100 for lodging, food and instruction for approximately forty children. The same allotment was given in the years 1875, 1876, and 1877. In 1878, the annual allotment was raised to $4,000, and was continued each year until 1890. From 1891 to 1900 inclusive, the Indian Department granted the sum of $12 50 per pupil per month, up to three hundred students, for their lodging, food, clothing, and instruction.

In 1875, the Fathers bought a printing press, for $1,000, which was shipped from Europe with the added charge of $400 for freight Accompanying the press in its journey to the northwest was Father Alexander Diomed, author of "New Indian Sketches" Father Diomed installed the press in the Mission and started its operation. He taught the Indian boys to set type, and in a year's time was printing a book of Bible stories in the language of the Kalispel, with 225 copies in the first edition The next project, a Kalispel language dictionary, took three years to print and contained 1136 pages.

The Mission Church, St. Ignatius

In 1890, the Ursuline nuns arrived at St. Ignatius, and established a kindergarten for the homeless orphans of the three tribes. Thus the Mission had three branches of schooling in operation: the girls' school by the Sisters of Providence; the Industrial and Agricultural School for Boys; and the kindergarten by the Ursulines.

In 1891, with the Mission growing rapidly, and in favor with the Indians, Father Rebmann appealed to his superiors for a new church to be built on the finest of Mission land. His appeal was answered, and a beautiful brick church was erected, one of the finest to be found anywhere. The interior of the church contains frescoes which entailed fourteen months of hard work by J. Carignano, a Coadjutor Brother of the Society of Jesus. This marvelous work is still admired annually by thousands.

26

Since 1900, the continuance of the work at the Mission has been a struggle. But one man whose impact was felt was Father Louis Taelman. Born in Belgium on April 19, 1866, Father Taelmann first came to the Mission in 1890, and as the years rolled on he returned again and again to work among the Indians He was the president of Gonzaga University from 1909 until 1913. Father Taelman was responsible for the building of the first church in Polson When the new church was completed, on October 5, 1910, Father Griva became its first resident priest When Father Taelman died, at the age of 95, in February, 1962, his last rites were performed at the St. Ignatius Catholic Church, where he had at one time been the chaplain.

Father Jerome D'Aste, a Jesuit priest, continued the work at the Mission from the latter part of 1890 until his death in 1910.

— **Protestant Missionaries** —

When the 1831 delegation of Indians attempted to interest missionaries in St. Louis, their mission was not immediately successful, but the impact was felt in the Protestant churches, namely the Methodist, Congregationalist, Dutch Reform, and the Presbyterian. David Thompson, a devout, religious man, was influential with the Indians and first drew their attention to the Bible. Another man who left his imprint with the Indians, hence their trip to St Louis, was Jedediah Strong Smith, an explorer and skilled adventurer in the wilds. He spent the winter of 1824 at the Saleesh House, and eventually aroused their curiosity in seeing "The White Man's Book of Heaven "

The Protestant missionaries responded at an earlier date than did the Black Robes, for in 1834, the Methodists

27

sent a well-equipped expedition to Oregon. Headed by Jason Lee and five associates, the group joined Nathaniel Wyeth's fur-trading caravan and left Independence, Missouri, on April 28, 1834. Jason Lee and his men were met at Green River, Wyoming, by a group of the Flatheads who had heard of the trip Analyzing the situation that appeared to prevail in the Montana territory, the early-day missionaries continued to Oregon, believing it to be a more fertile field for their work.

One of the earlier Protestant missionaries who did come to Montana was William Wesley Van Orsdel, a Methodist. Brother Van, as he was known throughout Montana, was born in Gettysburg, Pennsylvania. He left his home as a young man, in 1872, and headed west — to St. Louis and thence to Sioux City, Iowa. In Sioux City, he secured passage on the barge steamer, the "Far West," and headed up the Missouri River to the eastern part of Montana. The journey ended at Fort Benton where Brother Van held his first services in a saloon.

Brother Van was a good mixer with the frontiersmen and the Indians alike. In April, 1873, he held services near Choteau, in a log cabin of a Mr Howard, who had married a Piegan squaw. The service was attended by a few whites, some breeds, but primarily full-blooded Indians filled the small room. During the meeting, a roving band of Flatheads made a suprise attack and stole the horses of the worshippers. During the excitement, two horses were overlooked — one of them belonging to a teacher at the Blackfeet-Piegan Agency, and the other to Brother Van.

The irate Piegans gave chase on the two horses, and the Flatheads, thinking a large band was following them, abandoned their four-footed loot. The Piegan Indians, by

Methodists built first Protestant church on Reservation

way of thanking Brother Van, insisted that he join them in a buffalo hunt.

As one group of Indians ran the buffalo herd down the coulee, the main band of hunters attacked. Riding a spirited horse, Brother Van found himself at the head of the stampeding herd and was able to shoot a shaggy trophy. After the hunt, the women of the tribe skinned and dressed-out the buffalo, then prepared a feast for everyone.

Charles M. Russell, long a friend of Brother Van, painted a picture of the episode, and it now hangs in the reception room of the Deaconess Hospital in Great Falls, Montana.

Brother Van was a circuit rider and missionary for many years. His influence was felt, not only by the Indians, but by the early settlers for half a century. He was the center of attraction at the North Montana Methodist conference held at Polson in July, 1911.

CHAPTER FIVE
Indian Agents

Isaac Ingalls Stevens, born in North Andover, Massachusetts in 1818, was a man who left his imprint on the pages of the history of the northwest. Appointed the first governor of the newly-created Washington territory, which comprised western Montana, Governor Stevens entered this region in 1853 On September 24, 1853, he planted the American flag, and proclaimed the territory from the Continental Divide west to the Pacific Ocean, and from parallel 46 north to parallel 49, as the international boundary with Canada, to be under the civil territorial government of the United States.

At this time of history, there was a great deal of unrest among the Indians of the northwest. Governor Stevens was an ambitious man, anxious to make an impression and to have his name remembered in Washington. Although he realized the importance of fair dealing with the Indians, many of his agreements with them were never fully carried out by the federal government.

In 1854, Governor Stevens visited the St Ignatius Mission Shortly thereafter, he appointed Thomas Adams as a special Indian agent to prepare and arrange for a council with the chiefs of the three Indian tribes Many pow wows were held, and considerable work was done by Adams before a conference was arranged for July, 1855, to be held at Council Grove.

Attending this conference were Governor Stevens and several officials of the Indian department, Father Hoecken, and three Indian chiefs· Victor of the Salish (Flathead), Alexander of the Kalispel, and Michelle of the Kootenai Many meetings were held before an agreement was drawn up on July 16, 1855, and signed by all concerned By virtue of this treaty, the Flathead Reservation was designated for the exclusive use of the three tribes, known in the contract as The Confederated Tribes of Flatheads, Pend d'Oreilles and Kootenais

It was agreed that the Kalispell and Kootenai tribes would be located within the present boundaries of the Flathead Indian Reservation, and Chief Victor and his Flatheads would settle in the Bitter Root valley In this treaty, Victor ceded a large area, which is now western Montana, to the U S government Upon yielding the region, Victor insisted that his people retain that portion of the Bitter Root above Lolo Creek, but there was an alternate clause, the 11th article, which empowered the President to make surveys and to determine from those surveys whether it was better for the Flatheads to remain in the Bitter Root, or to be moved to the Jocko Agency

The treaty also provided that the three tribes were to be taught the white man's culture in farming, blacksmithing, carpentry, trades, and schools A saw mill, flour mill, and hospital would be established, and the U S. government would pay $120,000 in installments over a period of twenty years. An Indian agent would live among the Indians, and the Jesuits — the Black Robes — would instruct them in the various arts The Indians were to be supplied with the means to farm, and salaries and houses would be furnished the Chiefs

In the spring of 1856, Dr R H Landsdale, the first Indian agent, established the Jocko Agency That spring the Jesuit Fathers furnished some of the Indians with wheat seed and potatoes In May of that year, Dr. Landsdale went to Salt Lake City, via the Monida Pass route, and returned in June with an assistant, Henry G Miller. Mr Miller brought his wife to what was considered the wilds of the north As she was the first white woman to live in the midst of the Flatheads, they were amused to see her riding a horse side-saddle

Later that year, Major John Owen was transferred from St Mary's Mission to the Jocko as Indian agent, and assumed charge of the Indians in both the Flathead and Bitter Root valleys However, this plan did not prove feasible owing to the distance between St Mary's Mission (Fort Owen) and the Jocko In June, 1857, the agency at Jocko was closed and Major Owen returned to the headquarters at Fort Owen, and devoted all of his time to the Bitter Root

The government re-opened the Jocko agency in 1859, bringing in H M Chase as the Indian agent to supervise the work among the Kalispels and the Kootenais

Jet travel wasn't even a dream in a scientist's mind in those early days, the Pony Express carried the mail and the news of the era Slow as transportation was, Congress was even slower Six years after it was drawn up, on March 29, 1860, the Stevens' treaty was ratified by Congress.

The following month, after the treaty ratification, Major Owen was again returned to the Jocko agency, accompanied by two agricultural assistants, and the work went into high gear A store house, blacksmith shop, millwright shop and two houses were built, and a small farm was put into operation The first annuity payment was made to the Indians Farm machinery, stock and seeds were given to tribal members who were interested and capable of learning the white man's ways. The next year, a flour mill and a saw mill were erected by the government.

By 1871, the new superintendent Galbraith of the Jocko Agency reported, 105 farms on the reservation

33

were under cultivation. The Kalispels had seventy of the farms; the Flatheads had thirty-five. The Kootenai people weren't interested in farming — they settled in the Elmo and Dayton area, and lived on game, fish, roots, berries, and the inner bark of the yellow pine.

Into this scene of hustle and bustle, and apparent tranquility, came the white settlers, pushing into the Bitter Root valley rapidly and greedily. They petitioned the U.S. government to move the Flathead (Salish) Indians out of the Bitter Root A Presidential order was issued, decreeing that the Salish tribe should be moved to the Jocko, with $5,000 being appropriated to cover the cost of the move Chief Charlo, who had followed in the footsteps of his father, Chief Victor, as leader of the Salish people, began a fight that was to last twenty years. He refused to leave.

In 1872, the Government sent General James A. Garfield, accompanied by Lieutenants Viall and Claggett, to the Bitter Root to arrange a treaty covering the removal of Chief Charlo and his people. Garfield, in his report to the president, stated that he found the Flatheads unwilling to move because the government had never complied with the terms of the Hell Gate (Stevens) treaty.

Ambitious Garfield drew up another agreement between the government and the Indians This agreement provided for the removal of the Flathead tribe to the Jocko In return, the government would build sixty homes for them, 600 bushels of wheat would be delivered to the tribe the first year, the land would be broken and fenced for the Indians and they would be furnished with farm implements It was further agreed that the $5,000 appropriated for their removal would be given them directly, and that they would also receive $50,000, which would be

34

paid to them in ten equal installments The Indians would leave the Bitter Root as soon as the houses were built for them at Jocko. Those who preferred to remain could do so by taking up land in the Bitter Root in the regular prescribed manner.

This treaty was witnessed by government representatives, William H Claggett, D. G. Swain, W. F. Sanders, J A Viall, and Governor of Montana, B. F Potts. The marks of the Indian Chiefs were indicated to be those of Charlo, first Chief of the Flatheads; Arlee, second Chief; and Adolf, third Chief

The apparent duplicity outraged Chief Charlo He declared that he had never signed the treaty, he would never sign it in the future, and he would not move to the Jocko, nor would he urge his people to do so Even as houses were built at the Jocko, near the Agency, and Chiefs Arlee and Adolf and their following made the move from the Bitter Root valley, Chief Charlo remained adamant, and held his ground at Stevensville with his loyal Flatheads He stubbornly resisted all attempts to move him, stating that he hadn't signed the treaty and therefore was not bound by its provisions.

In 1873, Major Peter Ronan was appointed Superintendent of the Indian Agency Ronan was a shrewd, capable and energetic man, and under his administration the living conditions on the reservation began to improve. Although Major Ronan sympathized with Chief Charlo, he recognized the necessity of the chief and his people to leave the Bitter Root Their hunting grounds were gone, they were almost starving, and the continued settlement of the white people called for their removal

The matter was called to the attention of Congress, and an investigating committee composed of Senator

35

Vest of Missouri and Major Maginnis, Montana's delegate to Congress, was sent to the northwest. They heard Charlo's indignant story, and listened to Father Ravalli's version of the matter. Further investigation proved that the treaty did not bear Charlo's mark. Later, Garfield reported that he thought Charlo would go along with the other two chiefs when they readily agreed to the move to Jocko. His assumption was incorrect. Even after the investigation, Vest and Maginnis did their utmost to persuade the Chief to move, but they received an abrupt refusal. Adding Indian's insult to white man's injury, Chief Arlee was recognized by the government as the Chief of the Indians at the agency, and Charlo considered him to be a "renegade Nez Perce." Charlo was bitter and sore at heart, and vowed to die in the Bitter Root.

Several years passed, and in 1884, Major Ronan took Charlo and five of his sub-chiefs to Washington for a conference with the President and the Secretary of the Interior. Additional promises were made if Charlo and his people would move to the Jocko, but to no avail. It was finally agreed that the small tribe could remain in the Bitter Root as long as they were compatable with the white settlers. Compatibility was not a problem. Previous to this meeting, Chief Joseph and the tribe of Nez Perce attempted to induce Charlo and his people to join them in a raid on the white settlers. Charlo told him to look elsewhere for excitement and stay out of the Bitter Root.

Major Ronan continued in his attempt to win the friendship and trust of the embittered chief. A year later he noticed Charlo had softened a little when a distribution of food and supplies was made to the tribe.

As time went on, it became apparent that the Flatheads were not a success in farming, and their living conditions worsened. When Chief Arlee died, in 1891, General Carrington was sent to the Bitter Root in another attempt to persuade Charlo to move, hoping the death of Arlee would remove some of his grievous reasons for remaining. Charlo counseled with Major Ronan; he talked with Amos Buck, Stevensville merchant, and he finally made his decision.

"I will go — I and my children. My young men are becoming bad; they have no place to hunt. My women are hungry. For their sake, I will go. I do not want the land you promise. I do not believe your promises. All I want is enough ground for my grave. We will go."

On October 17, 1891, Charlo and his people — totaling less than three hundred — moved to the Jocko. The government built the old Chief a nice home in the square at the Agency.

A faint breeze ruffled a large banner of the Sacred Hearts of Mary and Jesus atop a tall pole as the weary Indians approached the church. Father P. Canistrelli, S.J., stood near the sacred emblem with out-stretched hands and blessed and welcomed them. Chief Charlo's countenance retained its usual expression of stubborn pride and sadness, as he advanced on foot and shook hands with all who were there to welcome him.

After the initial greeting, all assembled in the agency chapel to attend the benediction of the most Holy Sacrament. Following the benediction, Father Canistrelli, who had spent many years with the Flatheads addressed them in their own tongue with a sincere message of welcome.

Although Chief Charlo was content with the improved living conditions for his people, he was never reconciled to his new home. Charlo died, a proud chief, broken in health and spirit, on January 10, 1910.

A decision was made, in 1910, to move the Jocko Agency to a more central location on the reservation. Under Indian agent, Major Fred C. Morgan, the agency was moved to a site north of Dixon, adjacent and just east of the Flathead River. It became known as the Flathead Indian Agency, operating under the Bureau of Indian Affairs of the Department of the Interior.

Flathead Indian Agency at Dixon
(Meiers Studio Photo)

The Flathead Indian Agency, and the Tribal Council, have supervised all tribal business and affairs. Records, as of June 30, 1959, show that tribal and allotted lands, held in trust, amounted to 629,617.28 acres, much of which is in valuable forest. From the sales of timber products, rental from Kerr Dam, and other tribal sources, a per capita payment, ranging from $50 and up, is made in March of each year to members of the tribes. Total membership, more than doubled since 1910, is well over 5,000.

Ever since the white man entered the northwest, his influence has been of historical note No group of men had more influence on the advancement of the Indians than the Indian agents with their untiring efforts and sincere hopes for the future Following is a list of the agents who have served since 1873 —

Major Peter Ronan 1873-1892
Joseph T Carter 1893-1898
W H Smead 1898-1903
Major Samuel Bellew 1904-1908
Fred C Morgan 1908-1917
Theodore Sharp 1917-1920
F C Campbell 1920-1921
Charles E. Coe 1921-1934
L W. Shotwell 1934-1943
C C Wright 1943-1951
Forrest R Stone 1952-1957
Charles S Spencer 1957-1961
Presley T Labreche 1961-

William Irvine at his ranch   Charles Allard Sr.

Michel Pablo at his ranch
(Photo Courtesy of Josephine Browne)

CHAPTER SIX
Cattle Pioneers

Before the influx of settlers in the northwest, explorers and fur traders were the only white men to feast their eyes on the glorious beauty of the Flathead country. It was a land with an abundance of grass, fertile soil, cold and sparkling streams, and plenty of rainfall. It was ideal cattle country, and only sparsely grazed by wild horses and game.

The first cattle to enjoy this bovine heaven were brought in by fur traders to Fort Colville in 1850, to be used in bartering for horses with the Indians of the Jocko valley. The cattle were of low quality, but they served as a nucleus for the thriving cattle industry that was to eventually play an important role in the development of the reservation. Higher quality cattle were imported to the valley in 1855 by the Jesuit Fathers at the St. Ignatius Mission, and by the government at the Jocko agency.

In the 1860's and 70's, adventurous white men came to the northwest, seeking an elusive fortune. Many became discouraged with the hardships and moved on, but those who realized they couldn't get rich overnight, and had vision enough to see their future bright in the Flathead, remained and added a vast heritage to the country. Among them were: Angus McLeod, Sr.; Joseph Ashley, Sr.; Louis Clairmont; Camille Dupuis, Sr.; Alexander Morigeau, Sr.; Dave, Louis, and Octave Couture, Raphael Bisson, Louis Courville, Sr.; Joe Grenier, Sr.; Edwin Dubay; Joe Houle, Sr ; Jean B. Jette; Frank Jette; Isaac and Eli Pauline, Fred W. Glover, Sr.; August Finley, George Ledoux; Fred Roullier; Mike Matt; Joe Matt, Sr.; Garcon Demers, Bob Vinson — now living, 100 years old — and others All of these men were of high caliber — true pioneers. Raising cattle, grain, and horses, they played a vital part in the agricultural development of the Flathead. Many of their descendants — second, third, and fourth generations — live on the reservation at the present time.

Space does not permit us to relate the individual life histories of these men. We will, however, touch briefly on the lives of four men who were prominent pioneers of the reservation, and let their stories reflect the conditions and opportunities of the era.

— William Irvine —

William "Billy" Irvine was born at Post Creek, six miles north of the St. Ignatius Mission, on June 15, 1856. His father, Peter Irvine, was originally from Scotland and was employed by the Fort Connah trading post. Peter Irvine married a Flathead Indian woman, and the union was blessed with nine children, of which Billy was the eldest.

Billy was never formally educated, but graduated from the school of hard-knocks and experience. This type of education proved to be adequate in the early days of the northwest, and enabled him to eventually accumulate a vast estate in the latter part of the century.

As a young man he became an expert roper and top cowhand. His knowledge and traits of dependability and trustworthiness prompted other cattlemen of the valley to select him as trail boss for the first major cattle drive to a distant market.

On May 15, 1876, Billy Irvine and eleven tough cowhands started their herd of twelve hundred beef cattle toward Cheyenne Included in the caravan was a covered "chuck" wagon which was drawn by four oxen. The cattle were driven seven or eight miles a day on the free range, and allowed to rest at night. Half the crew would ride night-herd until midnight, when they were relieved by the other half of the crew.

The trail taken was routed through Missoula, Deer Lodge, the junction west of Butte, then through the Beaverhead, on to Bannack, Idaho Falls, across the treacherous Snake River, through the northeast corner of Utah, and into Wyoming; on to Laramie, and finally Cheyenne. This route was used to avoid the hostile Crow Indians who were on the warpath During the year of this first cattle drive, the Crows, led by Sitting Bull, staged the notorious massacre of General Custer and his army of 280 men.

The first major cattle market was in Ogden, but by grazing the big herd on to Cheyenne, it was possible to prime fatten the cattle, and also get them closer to the Chicago market without having to pay freight. By the time the four and five-year-old steers and cows reached Chicago, they would generally top the market.

Leaving Cheyenne on October 15th, the trail-weary cowhands arrived home in time for Christmas, with the hardships, trail-dust and discomforts behind them. Other trips, like the one described, followed in 1877, 1879, and 1880.

In 1878, Billy Irvine was hired by a prominent Deer Lodge stockman, Conrad Kohrs, to go to Davenport, Iowa, and return with two purebred horses for the Deer Lodge ranch Billy and his companion left the railroad at Corrine, Utah, with the horses, and made the trip overland in less than a month.

In the spring of 1881, Billy went north into the Alberta province and found work with the George Lane Cattle Company. He also worked for one of the largest cattle outfits in Canada, the Pat Bruns Company. In 1885, he

43

Reference to Indians on Line 11 should be to Sioux, not Crow.

was in charge of the cavalry horses for the Dominion of Canada during the Riell Rebellion.

Returning to the Flathead in 1886, he was staked to his first small herd — some three hundred head — by Charles Allard, Sr. Billy Irvine located his cattle ranch seventeen miles west of Polson, in a little valley between high hills. The pure water springs overflowed to the lower land that was ideal for pasture and hay, thereby sub-irrigating the fields.

In 1896, William Irvine married Emily Brown, a part-Indian woman of the Flatheads. She was an excellent helpmate for Billy — a true daughter of the Pioneers.

The Irvine herd, an excellent grade of white-face, grew and multiplied until it numbered over three thousand head by the early part of the 20th century. The ranch also carried a hundred head of western horses. Billy would make a shopping trip to Missoula twice a year, bringing back enough food supplies and ranch needs to last six months.

He was a good feeder, not only of livestock, but also of his men and family. This was attested to by his stepson, Arthur Larrivee, whom he raised to manhood Arthur weighed 260 pounds; he was so strong and big that in a wrestling match with "The Terrible Turk" he stayed for thirty minutes without being thrown.

Billy's close friends included Charles Allard, Sr. and Michel Pablo. He assisted Michel Pablo in the famous Pablo buffalo round-up in 1908-10 Following the round-up, Billy was given a fat buffalo cow, the hide of which was tanned and is still in existence at the old Irvine ranch. The present-day ranch is operated by Francis "Tat" Browne.

William "Billy" Irvine passed on to his reward at Polson on June 17, 1939. Josephine Browne and Emily Jorgenson, grand-daughters of Mrs. Irvine, live in Polson at the present time.

— Angus McDonald —

With the closing of the Fort Connah trading post in 1872, Angus McDonald returned to his ranch on the Flathead that he had established in 1847. The ranch was located about a mile south of Fort Connah, with the ranch building situated just west of Post Creek.

Angus McDonald prospered in the cattle business; at one time his herd numbered 2,000 head, and the ranch carried 200 horses. Remaining in the valley, his sons Tom, Joe, Duncan, and Angus C. also entered the livestock field and thrived. When the Northern Pacific Railway was built through Arlee, Ravalli, and Dixon, Duncan McDonald obtained a contract to furnish the road crews with beef, and the venture proved to be quite profitable.

The cattle king of the McDonald family proved to be Angus C. Locating in the Big Draw country, just inside the reservation boundaries, Angus C. and his sister, Margaret, raised a good grade of white-face cattle. According to their nephew, Charles McDonald, on one roundup they sold 2,200 head from their herd and still had enough cattle remaining to begin the foundation of another herd.

Angus McDonald is buried at the old homesite, one mile east and one mile north of the Post Creek store. He was a true pioneer with a vast heritage to leave his family There are many of his grandchildren living on the reservation at the present time. His grandson, Walter McDonald — youngest son of Joe — is a member of the Flathead Tribal Council and a past-president of this important governing board on the reservation. A fourth generation of the McDonalds is Joe, who is a member of the Hamilton High School faculty, and the football and basketball coach of the high school athletic teams.

— Charles Allard, Sr. —

One of the most colorful figures in the early day development of the reservation was Charles Allard, Sr. Born in Jarvis, Oregon in 1852, he was the son of Louis Allard, a Frenchman, who married a Cree Indian woman.

Father and son arrived in the Montana territory when Charles was ten years old, bringing with them a small herd of horses to be sold to the miners at the Bearmouth Mine, east of Hell Gate. When the herd had been sold, Louis Allard left his young son with friends, and set out for Idaho to replenish his stock. Young Charles learned later that his father had been mistaken for another man and was ambushed and killed by a Nez Perce Indian.

Charles went to work in the mines at Bearmouth, and also worked in the mines near Superior. In January, 1876, he married Emerance Brun (Brown), the youngest daughter of Louis Brun and the sister of Mrs William Irvine. Their first son, Joseph, was born in Frenchtown on November 11, 1876; and Charles, Jr. was born in 1878.

The Allard family moved to the reservation, and located their cattle ranch about four miles southwest of the present town of Pablo. From 1882-83, Allard furnished beef to railroad crews building the tracks that would eventually bring more people into his beloved country. In those days, the beef cattle were driven to the crew camps and slaughtered for use. In these herding operations, Charles Allard was assisted by his son, Joseph.

His wife, Emerance, passed away in 1887, at the age of 26. Six years later he married Louise Courville, a daughter of Louis Courville, Sr. Two daughters were born of this union; surviving is Eva May Allard, who is presently a registered nurse in San Francisco, California.

The life of Charles Allard was ended abruptly at the age of 44. While riding the range, looking after his stock, he struck his right knee against a tree. The injury worsened, and he was treated in a Missoula hospital. Home care and more hospital treatment failed to bring about any improvement, and Allard went to Chicago where the knee cap was removed. His constitution was not strong enough to withstand the effects of the operation, and he died shortly thereafter.

— Michel Pablo —

Little is known of the early boyhood of Michel Pablo other than he was of Spanish descent and was born at Fort Benton, Montana, in 1846. It is related on seeemingly reliable authority that Michel and his brother, Laurette, were the only survivors of an Indian raid on the white settlement at Fort Benton. Michel's first memory, after the skirmish, was of being wrapped in a buffalo robe in the company of the Blackfeet Indians.

In 1864, he gained employment on the cattle ranch of Angus McLeod, near Arlee, and remained there for two years Fluent in English and Indian languages, he was employed by the Jocko agency as an interpreter, and continued in this capacity until 1870.

At this time, he moved to the lower Flathead valley, and established what was later to become the Pablo Cattle and Buffalo Ranch. This ranch was two miles south of the present town of Pablo, which was later named in his honor Michel Pablo married an Indian woman, Agette Finley, in 1866, and their family included three sons and three daughters Louis, Joseph, and Alexander; Annie,

47

who married Orson Dupuis; Margaret, later the wife of John Ashley; and Mary, who was wed to Tony Barnaby.

With astute management and hard work, Michel's ranch grew and prospered, and he became known throughout western Montana as the cattle-king of the lower Flathead. At the peak of ranch production, in 1906-07, there were approximately 10,000 head of cattle grazing on the pastures and ranges controlled by Michel Pablo. (A member of the family estimated that there were 30,000 head of cattle on the ranch at one time, and added the information that the grass was so high, when a cow laid down to chew her cud, she was completely hidden from view. It is thought that the estimate of the cattle is a lot like that grass — too high.)

Michel Pablo never lived to see the townsite, later named for him, become a thriving community. He died at the family home on July 12, 1914.

CHAPTER SEVEN
Buffalo Days
— The Pablo-Allard Buffalo —

As the wind howled in the night and the storm increased its fury, Walking Coyote, a half-breed Indian, felt the storm within himself abate. He shuddered as he looked at the body at his feet. His wife was dead It would be difficult to explain to her people at the St. Ignatius Mission that he had shot her because of the furies in his head; better not wait to explain Better get on the horse and ride across the mountains to start a new life.

Walking Coyote rode into his new life when he entered the Blackfoot Indian Reservation He took unto himself a new wife, but still was not content with his new surroundings. He missed the mountains and streams of the Flathead country. Perhaps time would make the Flathead people forget what he had done, and he could safely return, but a man could never be sure.

He lived among the Blackfeet for two years, always yearning for something more to view than stretching plains Noticing his melancholy state, some of the Blackfeet braves suggested that he capture a few buffalo from the plains he hated so much, and take them to the Flathead as a sort of peace offering No buffalo existed on the Flathead reservation, and perhaps he would be forgiven for his crime, and be hailed as a hero, if he could successfully transplant the buffalo from the plains to the mountain valley.

In 1873, Walking Coyote managed to capture his buffalo — two bulls and two heifers He worked with them patiently and almost religiously, they were the return-trip ticket to his homeland When the wild animals reached the point where they would follow the

49

horses as if they were colts, he felt they were ready. In the spring of 1874, Walking Coyote, his new wife, and the four buffalo started the trek across the mountains to the valley of the Missions

Just as the Blackfeet had foretold, Walking Coyote was forgiven He happily took up his life again on the Flathead His meager herd of buffalo expanded as the years and Mother Nature took their natural course. By 1884, there were thirteen head of buffalo, and Walking Coyote held a certain amount of prestige among his people.

The white man soon saw the possibilities in a herd of buffalo Angus McDonald, formerly a fur trader and now in the cattle business, began negotiations with Walking Coyote to buy his herd Before the deal could be closed, Walking Coyote received another offer from Charles Allard and Michel Pablo He gave much thought to the offer from the white men, and finally agreed to sell to Allard and Pablo on the condition that he be paid in currency only — nothing but green paper money would do

Walking Coyote met the two men under a big pine tree not far from their cattle ranches He watched as they counted the money — ten dollar bills placed in stacks of ten As each stack of one hundred dollars was completed, a rock was placed on top of it to prevent the breeze from scattering the green backs over the valley It was quite a task, and consumed quite a bit of time As the stacks of money and rocks lined out across the area, a small squirrel climbed out of the pine tree and scampered playfully through the currency Completely distracted, Allard and Pablo gave chase, caught the squirrel and killed it, then sheepishly returned to the task at hand.

Walking Coyote nervously eyed the money, and fidgeted until the transaction was completed. He tossed the rocks aside, scooped up the $3,000 from the ground, and hurriedly left. Charles Allard and Michel Pablo now owned a herd of buffalo.

Taking his small fortune to Missoula, Walking Coyote began a celebration that lasted for several days. His popularity increased with each day as more and more friends joined the merry-making. But the party was soon over. Walking Coyote was found dead under the north end of the Higgins Avenue bridge . . his final furies were spent — and so was the $3,000

In 1893, a portion of the Allard-Pablo buffalo herd was put on exhibition at the World's Fair in Chicago, and created quite a stir of interest. A mutual interest in buffalo brought about the meeting of Charles Allard and Buffalo Jones in Chicago. Jones, who owned a ranch near Omaha, Nebraska, had recently purchased buffalo in Manitoba, Canada. The two buffalo-fanciers began negotiations which were completed a year later with the delivery in Butte of 26 head of purebred buffalo and 18 head of hybrids — known as catalo

Allard met Buffalo Jones and the newly-purchased herd in Butte He took with him Michel Pablo, cowboys, and plenty of enthusiasm, but not enough money to close the deal Senator W. A. Clark, whose brother, J A Clark, had worked as a cook on the Allard ranch the year before, made a short term loan to Allard, and the purchase from Buffalo Jones was completed

The herd of buffalo was driven overland from Butte to the Flathead valley by the new owners and their cowboys. The catalo were turned out on Wild Horse Island so they wouldn't cross-breed with the pure bred buffalo.

51

By 1896, at the time of Charles Allard's death, the herd numbered three hundred. Michel Pablo retained his share of the herd, 150 head, but the heirs of the Allard estate decided to liquidate their share. The buffalo were divided equally between the widow, Louise Allard, and the four children, Joe, Charles, Jr., Eva May, and Anna Louise Joe Allard sold his share to Charles Conrad, a Kalispell banker; Charles and his sisters sold their buffalo to Howard Eaton of Wolf, Wyoming; and Mrs. Allard's buffalo were purchased by Judge Woodrow of Missoula. Judge Woodrow later sold them to the Miller Brothers' 101 Ranch in Bliss, Oklahoma.

In 1906, the U.S. Government was preparing to open the Flathead Indian Reservation for homestead entry. With the possibility of homesteaders over-running the reservation by 1910, Pablo entertained the thought of selling his vast herd

Michel Pablo had no actual knowledge of how many head he owned inasmuch as they were scattered over a wide area, mostly west of the Pend d'Oreille river. A buyer from Canada inspected portions of the herd and returned north to interest the Canadian government in purchasing the buffalo. Negotiations were transacted through the offices of the Canadian National Park at Banff, Alberta, of which Howard Jones was the superintendent. He was assisted by Alex Ayotte, head of the Dept. of Immigration in the State of Montana. A deal was finally consummated whereby Canada was to receive the entire herd, delivered on stock cars at Ravalli, for the sum of $200,000.

With the Canadian government's purchase of the entire herd of over 600 head of the Pablo buffalo in 1906, the next order of business for Michel Pablo was the round-

ROUNDUP RIDERS — This picture was taken near the home ranch during the Pablo buffalo roundup. From left are Charles M. Russell, famous Montana cowboy artist; Marcel Michell, Joe McDonald, unidentified, Jim Michell, Luizo Ashley, Alec Pablo, Don Michell, Alec Ashley, Louie Pablo, Joe Pablo, Arthur Ray and Michel Pablo.

up. Special corrals were built at Ravalli for the loading of the buffalo into reinforced stock cars of the Northern Pacific Railroad. From Ravalli, the buffalo would travel over five different railways to reach their destination of Wainwright, Alberta, Canada — a distance of 1,200 miles.

In the spring of 1907, Pablo constructed a set of corrals at his ranch headquarters, two miles south of what is now the town of Pablo. He hired twenty-five of the best cowboys available on the reservation, and the mammoth roundup began.

Whenever possible, the cows and calves were separated from the bulls and were driven overland to the Ravalli loading corrals The bulls were retained in the corrals at ranch headquarters and then loaded into wagons with strongly-built racks. These racks were ten feet high, well-braced, and built for hard wear, and were just wide enough for one buffalo bull to stand in.

Some of the bulls weighed as much as 2,200 pounds, and the idea of corrals, racks and wagons was completely alien to them Their reactions were frequently violent, resulting in many narrow escapes of life for both horses and riders. After a summer of extreme hard work, less than a hundred head had been placed f o.b. at the railhead in Ravalli The roundup was abandoned.

Charles Allard, Jr., raised with the buffalo since boyhood, persuaded Michel Pablo to reconsider. Knowing the ways of buffalo, and the lay of the land, he felt confident that he could finish the job and deliver all of the herd to Ravalli and the stock cars. Disliking the taste of defeat, Pablo put Charles Allard, Jr , in complete charge of the operation.

With this responsibility resting squarely on his shoulders, Charles set to work immediately with the con-

54

Rounding up buffalo is no easy chore!

Captured buffalo were hauled in special wagons

struction of a new set of corrals just east of the sharp bend in the Pend d'Oreille river, above Sloan's ferry. This site was fifteen miles closer to Ravalli than the corrals at ranch headquarters. Two sides of the corrals were built down to the edge of the river to a comparatively narrow width The first corral covered about five acres of ground, and was connected to small corrals and a loading chute.

Across the river, a sturdy linefence was built, running west along the ridge of the big hill for a distance of 26 miles Most of the buffalo were in the hills west of the river, and the lay of the hills across the river was ideal for herding as they diagonally came to a narrow point at the water The buffalo were gathered, and herded through this natural chute to the water's edge, and made to ford the river When they climbed out of the water, on the east side, they walked right into the newly constructed corral, and were headed for Ravalli, stock cars, and Canada By the time this plan was worked out to perfection, it was well along into the summer of 1908

Then the work began in earnest The cows, calves, and younger bulls were easier to herd into the traps set for them, but with the older and heavier bulls it was another story All too often, the men would start with a large gathering of buffalo, the bulls would break away time and again, and when they arrived at the river there would only be ten or fifteen head corralled And so it went during the season — hard work, frustrating work, and dangerous work

The big roundup continued through the year 1909, and on into 1910 It was recorded in The Flathead Courier of August, 1910, that the smoke was so condensed from a forest fire raging around Wallace, Idaho, that it was nec-

56

essary for Allard and his men to abandon the roundup until after the smoke had lifted.

The buffalo roundup attracted wide attention, both in this country and in Canada, attracting photographers and noted men who traveled many miles to record the rendezvous with the shaggy animals. The big bulls charged man or beast at the slightest provocation — many believed they did it for fun. Photographers often had their cameras smashed in the melee, but fortunately none lost their lives.

Michel Pablo set up a big camp for the working crew, and kept the bean pot bubbling for his men and the visitors. Among his guests who enjoyed the hospitality and excitement were old friends, Billy Irvine and Duncan McDonald. In 1909, Charles M. Russell, noted cowboy artist, spent some time at the river bend headquarters, and sketched many paintings of the colorful spectacle.

On Aug. 18, 1910, The Flathead Courier reported that there were seventy-five to eighty head of the biggest and most dangerous buffalo yet to be corralled. Joe Marion was in charge of this task These buffalo were very cunning and could outrun the fastest horse.

Twenty-five head of the unruly buffalo had to be killed, and Pablo sold the hides for robes, and gave the tough meat to the Indians. Johnny McDonald, one of the surviving riders of the roundup, stated that there was only one big bull which was able to get out of the sturdy, high corrals at Ravalli. When he did, he almost ran over a buggy in which Mrs. George Beckwith of St. Ignatius was riding. It is believed that her young son, Phil, was with her at the time. There was also one buffalo that crashed through the side of a stock car and had to be killed.

The final shipment, seven head, was made on June 1, 1912, making the grand count near 700 head. Their new home contained 123,000 acres of pasture. This was the largest transfer of buffalo from one country to another that had ever transpired.

The riders who survived this historic roundup, and are living at the present time, are Johnny McDonald and Marion Deschamps of St. Ignatius; Walter Sloan of Hot Springs; Jim Grinder of Missoula; Fred Houle of Pablo.

In 1961, memories of the earlier buffalo roundup were revived when Ike Melton of Hot Springs sold his herd of about 180 head of buffalo, and shipped them to Gillette, Wyoming.

Ike's Whiskey Trail ranch was the scene of the old west restored as thirty riders hit the trails to bring in the wily creatures whose dispositions and attitudes toward man hadn't changed in fifty years. Riders were charged, treed, and given a bad time in general; horses were ridden hard and fast, and knew they had put in a day's work when they were unsaddled at night.

In direct contrast to the Pablo roundup, which began in 1907 and finished in 1912, the Melton roundup started in the latter part of September, 1961, and the final head was shipped in February, 1962 There weren't as many animals involved, but the modern-day facilities and transportation eliminated many of the headaches encountered by the earlier-day buffalo-hands

Cowboys who took part in the Melton roundup included Bill Gould, Gary Abbey, Noel Vincent, Dick Gardner, Paul Gardner, Bob and Tide Darlington, Ben Haight, Jim Jackson, LaRue Melton, Larry Christenson, Gerald Leighton, Dale Ogden, Stan Harris, Al Anderson, John

Scott, Kenny Piedalue, Jim Ely, Cecil Mocabee, Lloyd Pettit, Leon Melton, Slim Coppedge, Dwight and Del Nicholson, Tiny Powell, Bill Phillips, Ed Bratton, Virgil Dutton, and Paul Evans.

— The National Bison Reserve —

The National Bison Reserve, located in the lower part of the reservation, is a major point of interest for tourists in the northwest during the summer months. Guides conduct daily tours through the reserve, which not only feature the buffalo but also fifty to seventy-five elk, nearly three hundred mule deer, approximately one hundred white-tailed deer, twenty-five to thirty-five big-horn sheep, and twelve to twenty-five prong-horn sheep It is also a haven for nutcrackers, magpies, woodpeckers, meadow larks, horned owls, prairie falcons, goshawks, coyotes and bobcats

The buffalo and wild game refuge was established in 1908 by Congress at the request of President Theodore Roosevelt It comprises nearly 19,000 acres of land which consists of high hills, buttes, and rolling ground The area is surrounded by twenty-three miles of high, strong, woven-wire fence Congress appropriated $40,000 for the cost of the reserve, and it was paid to the Flathead Indians

The American Bison Society raised more than $10,000 by popular subscription to buy the animals that originally stocked the range Forty-one head of buffalo constituted the foundation herd Thirty-four head were purchased from the Charles Conrad estate (The foundation stock of the Conrad herd were originally purchased from the estate of Charles Allard, Sr , in 1896) Seven head of bison were donated, two from Montana, two from Texas, and three from New Hampshire °

At the present time, there are 342 head of buffalo on the reserve. Approximately 100 calves are born each year, from the latter part of April through June. These calves are used as replacements in the herd. In an effort to maintain a herd of consistent size, approximately 100 head of buffalo are butchered in November of each year, and the meat is sold by the quarter to lucky number holders who previously registered for the drawing during the summer.

Buffaloes are sturdy, hardy animals, and on the range are never domesticated. Consequently at times they will charge a man or horse without reason, just as they did before the advent of fences. They never require hay, but live in the hills the year 'round. There is a wide variance in the weight of the male and the female buffalo. The bull will range in weight from 1,800 to 2,200 pounds, and the cows will weigh from 900 to 1,200 pounds.

Buffaloes have a heavy coating of hair, especially on the front half of the body. This pelage is a protection against the cold in the winter and against the heat in the summer. They are unable to turn over when they roll due to the big hump on the forefront of their backs. During the hot summer months, they stay out of the sun as much as possible and wallow quite a lot in their favorite wallowing holes.

The National Bison Range at Moiese gained fame in 1933 when a male albino (white) buffalo was born. This rare buffalo, named Big Medicine, was pure white except for the wooly knob between his horns. He was born of a cow of normal color. Big Medicine sired another white buffalo, which was born in May, 1937. His offspring, who was blind, had pink eyes and even white hooves, and was sent to the National Zoological Gardens in Washington,

Big Medicine, world famous albino patriarch of National Bison Range (Meiers Studio Photo)

D.C., in December, 1937. It was on exhibition there until its death in 1949.

Big Medicine has been seen and photographed by thousands of people, having been kept in an exhibition pasture with a small number of other buffalo, near the headquarters. He died in 1959. At one time, during the first half of the 1800's, it is estimated that the buffalo population numbered about 60 million head, but in all of this countless number of buffalo, not more than ten or eleven white buffalo were ever in existence.

C. J. Henry is the present manager of the National Bison Reserve. Cy Young was the Range Foreman from 1937 to 1959, when he was seriously injuried by a high voltage line. Victor May has since been Range Foreman.

At the present time, the reservation can boast of two other small herds of buffalo. Bob Schall, who has a ranch three miles west of Arlee, has a foundation herd of sixteen. Bill Gould also has sixteen head of buffalo on his ranch, which is fifteen miles southwest of Polson, in the southern part of Valley View. These men take their surplus buffalo to California each year for the Christmas trade.

Allard Stage with Joe Allard at reins
(Photo Courtesy of Joe Allard)

Auto Stage with Tom Parsons at the wheel
(Herman Schnitzmeyer Photo)

CHAPTER EIGHT
Land Transportation

In the early part of the 1800's, roads were unheard of on the reservation. Trails cut through the wilderness, connecting one piece of civilization with another. These trails were created by the repetitious footfalls of horses, Indians, and wild animals.

One of the earliest modes of transport, concocted for convenience, was a type of u-haul trailer. Indian squaws fashioned it with two long poles and the hide of a buffalo or other wild animal. The hide was stretched between the poles and fastened down; the poles were then attached to either side of a horse and the conveyance was ready for hauling

In 1845, when the Black Robes came into western Montana, two-wheel carts and four wheel wagons were introduced to the transportation system. As the reservation developed, with the establishment of the missions and the opening of the agency at the Jocko, wagon trails were used extensively for the transportation of provisions, annuity goods, and farm machinery from the agency to the Indians.

The main "highway" through the reservation began at the Jocko Agency and bumped its way to Ravalli. Up the big hill from Ravalli, where it had been cut and chipped with plows, crude scrapers, and road drags, the wagon trail coarsed its way to St. Ignatius, by-passing the Mission by a short distance. Avoiding hills wherever possible, the road wound north to Ronan Springs and on through what is now Pablo Then north and west it rambled, topping a hill and giving the wagon driver his first view of the Flathead Lake as he rolled directly north into Lambert's Landing (earlier called "Foot of the Lake," and now known as Polson).

There were no bridges to speak of, even as late as 1910, between Polson and Ravalli. At Ronan, where the spring was unsafe to cross, planks were thrown across the high water for passage. Crossing all streams and creeks, especially Post Creek at high water time, was quite a feat. Rainy weather brought its problems, too, adding mud to the ruts, and making it next to impossible to turn out from the road. Turning off the road was often necessary, especially if any oncoming traffic was encountered.

With the main line of the Northern Pacific through the southern part of the reservation in 1883, and the settling of the northern section of the reservation, the opportunity and need of a passenger and freight service was noted and shortly put into operation. A light wagon or hack carried the pay load as far north as Demersville. By 1888, Charles Allard, Sr , had established a mail and passenger line from Ravalli to Demersville, crossing the river at Lambert's Landing by ferry It took four days for the round-trip. In 1889, Allard added another passenger and mail run on the east side of the Flathead Lake, with an over-night stop at Station Creek — the present home of Dr. J L. Richards

From 1889 until 1892, business was brisk in the freight and passenger line Competition between stage lines often brought benefits to the customers An old-time stage operator attempted to compete with the Allard line With a mail-carrying contract to pay his expenses, Allard could afford to offer his passengers a free ride, with dinner thrown in as an extra. His competitor, without the U.S. backing, didn't compete long.

With the impending opening of the reservation to white settlement, traffic demands increased and a 14-passenger Concord stage was put on the run in July, 1908, an continued until November, 1909. (This Concord stage is presently owned by the Con F. Kelly estate at Swan Lake, and was on exhibition during the Golden Jubilee in the summer of 1960) Joe Allard, the stage driver, left Ravalli at 6.30 A.M., driving four horses in good weather and six horses when the roads were bad. He changed horses at Post Creek and again at Ronan, arriving in Polson at noon The return trip began at 12 30, and the horses were headed for the barn at Ravalli around 4:30 P M

In 1910, the G W Williams Transportation Company was awarded the mail contract, and took over the stage run between Ravalli and Polson During the summer of 1910, the mail volume became so heavy for the regular horse stage that Tom Bateman, president of the company, put on a team and wagon for the mail route. This slower method of mail delivery, which took an entire day, dissatisfied the mail patrons along the line at Mission, Leon, Ronan, and Polson When the volume of mail lessened, their quick service was returned

On April 25, 1910, Robert F Vinson, who celebrated his 100th birthday at Polson in 1961, started the operation of a stage line between Polson and Dixon and returned on a daily schedule This continued through 1910 and 1911, going through much of the land that was open for homestead — Ronan, townsite of Tabor (now Charlo), Moiese, and Dixon Mr. Vinson also operated a stage line between Polson and Somers at this time.

Two auto stage lines competed for their share of the business from Polson to Ravalli. Frank Latimer operated a Stevens-Duryea which carried seven passengers, and "Si" Sawyer put his seven-passenger Reo into the transportation business The fare on all stages was $5 00, one-way, but autos were not too dependable, especially in the winter time or on muddy roads

On May 25, 1912, a twelve-passenger auto stage was put on the Ravalli-Polson run by the Williams Transportation Company This auto stage was faster than horses. On a trial run, from St Ignatius to Ronan, it was clocked at the phenomenal speed of eighteen miles in one hour and sixteen minutes The horses were turned out to pasture for the summer, but the auto-stage, a Glide, proved to be an expensive substitute The stage required six new tires each month, and these tires had to be ordered from the factory in Peoria, Illinois, and cost $390.

The driver of this modern mode of transportation was Tom Parsons, who now lives on a ranch in Irvine Flats Due to the road conditions, he drove the auto in the summer and the horses in the winter.

One morning, on a winter run, he headed south from Ronan with one passenger, a large man who sat next to him in the "boot," huddled in his fur coat. As the stage headed down-grade, north of Post Creek, the horses spooked and plunged headlong out of control. The front wheel of the stage went cross-wise in a rut, jarring the coach in its mad dash. As Tom strained to control the horses, he glanced out of the corner of his eye to see how his passenger was faring, and caught a startled glimpse just as the large man disappeared out of sight, over the edge of the stage When the horses tired of running in the snow, Tom turned the stage around and returned for his passenger He found him standing beside a large hole, dozed out of the deep snow, and brushing the excess off his fur coat The lone passenger was the famous German photographer, Herman Schnitzmeyer

In the days when Polson was known as "Pied de lai" or "Foot of the Lake," crossing the river required a ride on a ferry boat which was operated by Baptiste Eneas. In April of 1910, with a much greater demand for crossing the river, the building of the Polson bridge was begun Polson, at that time, was in Flathead County and a large amount of the cost of the bridge was raised by popular subscription.

The construction of the longest wagon bridge in the state was started from the west side of the river The plans called for it to connect on the east side with B Street (now 2nd Avenue and U S Highway 93) This plan suited everyone on B Street, but the merchants on C Street (now 3rd Avenue) objected strenuously, and served an injunction on the contractors They insisted that C Street was more toward the center of town (To B, or not to B, soon became the question) Violent arguments ensued over the controversy, with merchants from both streets claiming priority due to a more favorable position At one time, the businessmen got so hot under the collar over the issue that eight of them were put in jail to cool off All of the lawyers in Polson, and two from Ronan, were kept busy just serving legal papers

Farmers and ranchers who lived across the river finally brought the problem to a head They had to pay 50c for a one-way ferry trip. and they made their displeasure felt A compromise was reached Each street would have an approach to the bridge, with the businessmen from both streets paying the additional cost, $1,020

On August 18, 1910, the first wagon crossed the river on the new bridge, and both approaches were completed and open to the public on August 29th

Early Polson bridge had twin approaches on city side
(Thiri Aerial View Photo)

The twin-approach bridge served faithfully until June 8, 1927, when the present bridge was constructed. The W. P Roscoe Company of Billings erected the bridge at a cost of $101,116.27 The new bridge had one approach

Soon after the opening of the reservation in 1910, rumors were afoot from time to time concerning the building of a railroad through the area. Most of the lines were built on paper or dream clouds, and they invariably went from Ravalli to Kalispell, connecting the Northern Pacific to the Great Northern In 1911, two electric lines were planned for each side of the lake, joining at Polson before continuing on to Ravalli In 1912, it was rumored that the W A Clark interests of Butte would build an electric line from Missoula to Polson. Surveys were made of the proposed line, but that was the end of it.

Transportation on both land and water was a grave problem to a growing reservation In Polson, the merchants had to lay in stocks of merchandise that would suffice until spring owing to the prohibitive freight rates by stage. It was a day of celebration when the first boat could come across the lake after the spring break-up For many years, the Wade Clothing Company presented a brand-new "Curlee" suit of clothes to the man who came the nearest in estimating the exact time that the Polson Bay was clear of ice.

In 1913, the Northern Pacific Railway made surveys of the area, and in the early part of 1914, bonds were sold to a firm in New York City. But war clouds appeared and obliterated the plans, so the proposed railroad from Dixon to Polson was postponed. In 1916, the right-of-way for the railroad was secured, and in 1917, work was begun on laying the track out of Dixon. The last spike was driven in Polson by noon on December 9, 1917. This was a time of rejoicing. The Polson depot was jammed with people, who happily listened to speeches. After the speechmaking, the crew was treated to a turkey dinner at the Grandview Hotel by the Chamber of Commerce. Full-time service was established in August, 1918, and was a great boon to business throughout the reservation.

Freight and passenger trains operating between Missoula and points on the reservation were drawn by steam engines. The passenger trains carried the mail, passengers, and express every day except Sunday, making the round-trip every twenty-four hours. Later this service was reduced to a mixed freight and passenger train which was drawn by diesel motor. The train was affectionately called

Northern Pacific bus on today's Polson-Missoula run

Mr. and Mrs. Joe Allard during Golden Jubilee of Reservation opening, 1960. This is same stage Mr. Allard drove in 1909 (Meiers Studio Photo)

"the Galloping Goose." "The Galloping Goose" made its last passenger run on February 28, 1935, and another page of history was turned.

Great changes have since taken place in the transportation field. Except for carload lots, railway freighting and passenger service has been eliminated from the scene. Mammoth trucks with semi-trailers carry provisions, annuity goods, farm machinery, and other staples of life over paved super-highways that were, at one time, dusty trails traveled by a squaw with her own version of a semi-trailer.

This squaw could look to the heavens and her eyes would embrace the azure blue of a clear sky or one dotted with floating clouds. People of today, who travel this trail, are often moving too fast to notice the sky — unless it happens to have a jet-stream in it. Then they wonder how long it will be before a man is landed on the moon.

CHAPTER NINE
Traffic On Flathead Lake

The shortest distance between two points is a straight line. That geometrical fact has been drummed into school children for decades. With the early pioneers it was applied in good fashion along with a large amount of common sense The shortest route through the reservation, to Kalispell and points north, was across the Flathead Lake The roads on either side of the lake left a lot to be desired so the traveling public took to boats, considering them the best available transportation

The demand was soon met with the supply as the first boat of any consequence was built in 1883 by Neil and George Nelson and Fred Lindgren. Named "The Swan," this twenty-ton sail boat made the run from Lambert's Landing (Polson) to Dooley's Landing, at the north end of the lake, and return, in one week's time This boat handled all of the freight and passenger business In 1885, the business was sold to Captain Mathew Kerr who re-named the boat "The U S. Grant," and installed a steam engine to power it With the increased power and speed, Captain Kerr was able to make two trips each week, and eventually, with the installation of improved machinery, a round trip was made every two days

In 1886, Duncan McDonald and Mr Briggs formed a partnership, and brought in a new boat from the east. Christened "The Pocohontas," it was larger than "The U S Grant," and of more modern design Freight traffic had increased to such an extent that both companies were able to operate in the black

In September of 1887, "The Pocohontas" was returning from the north with forty tons of freight and a roster of passengers Seeking to avoid high waves in a sudden storm, it ran aground between the lake shore and Melita Island. All of the passengers escaped injury, but the forty tons of freight went to the bottom of the lake. It was later recovered, but "The Pocohontas" had seen its last days of multiple service. In 1888, the craft was raised, remodeled, and converted into a freight barge.

The next boat of any size to cruise the waters of the Flathead was "The Tom Carter," named for the Montana U.S senator. Built in 1889 at Demersville, the capacity of this craft was thirty thousand pounds, which could be made up of freight or passengers, or a combination thereof During the years 1890-1892, with the construction of the Great Northern Railway through Kalispell, "The Tom Carter" carried its full share on the Flathead. Existing records show a pasenger list of 586 and freight bills totaling forty tons.

In April, 1891, as labor and materials were being brought through the reservation for the railway construction in the north, "The Crescent" was brought into service. "The Crescent" could carry one hundred passengers and seventy-five tons of freight; it featured two staterooms and had stables for ten horses. Measuring sixteen feet wide and 150 feet long, "The Crescent" could draw sixteen inches of water The stern wheeler was a mammoth nineteen feet in diameter.

Even larger and more elaborate than "The Crescent" was "The Montana" Partially built in Portland, Oregon, and shipped to the Flathead by Captain Kerr in 1891, this boat was also 150 feet long, but was 26 feet wide, and drew eighteen inches of water "The Montana" was manned by a crew of twenty-five, which looked after 150 passengers and 150 tons of freight There were eighteen staterooms on board, in addition to a bar and ladies' and men's rooms.

During the construction of the Great Northern Railway, freight became so congested at the Ravalli railhead, awaiting transfer north, that J. D. Heyfron of Missoula, contractor for the transportation, had 200 teams and wagons hauling from Ravalli to the Flathead and the boats.

When the railway through Kalispell was completed, business on Flathead Lake plummeted The only boats of any size running on the lake were of fifty-ton capacity or less. These included "The Eva B," "The Queen," and "The Mary S."

In 1910, when the Flathead Reservation was opened to homesteaders, business boomed again, and the rush was on to get boats into the water Captain Eugene Hodge launched the "New Klondyke" on May 27, 1910. This boat, a stern wheeler, was 120 feet long, 26 feet wide, drew thirty inches of water and had a carrying capacity of 425 passengers and 118 tons of freight It featured four staterooms and a dining room.

"The Montana," owned by the Flathead Lake Navigation Company, was in service in 1910, and had a carrying capacity of 160 passengers and 40 tons of freight.

The fastest big boat on the lake was "The City of Polson," which was launched June 15, 1910, by the East Side Navigation Company It was powered by two gas engines, and was covered with boiler plate which was used for ice-breaking in the winter Carrying 75 passengers and 19 tons of freight, "The City of Polson" was 61 feet long and 12 feet wide

"The Big Fork," a large barge, was used exclusively for freight and for breaking ice in the winter. Running the bow up on the ice, the barge would break through with its heavy weight However, when 'old man winter' was at his best, there wasn't much "The Big Fork" could do about the ice Lake traffic halted.

Polson merchants preferred shipping by water transport because overland freighting, with wagons or sleds, proved to be too expensive. Freight from Polson to Somers, a distance of 35 miles by water, was 10c per cwt Freight from Polson to Ravalli, a distance of 35 miles by land, was 50c per cwt Consequently, merchants took their major shipments of goods in the fall, to stock up for the winter months when the lake was impassable for boats.

Most of the livestock from the Polson territory was shipped, via barges, to Somers where it was loaded on Great Northern stock cars for shipment to market. In 1915, a bumper-crop year, 417,000 bushels of grain were shipped by barge from the two elevators at Polson. The registry of boats showed that twenty boats had a total capacity of 1,023 passengers and 900 tons of freight daily in 1915.

Pleasant memories of "the good old days" stem from this particular era — the growth of a community with its hustle and bustle; the arrival and departure of the lake boats with the accompanying excitement; and perhaps best of all—County Fair time at Kalispell The entire county turned out for the fair, and the boats carried the crowd Fun and merriment echoed across the waters as the pioneers relaxed and enjoyed life at its best

One memory, which highlighted the boat trip to the fair for many, was watching a small man scramble up and down a 30 foot cable which stretched from the Captain's cabin to the middle point of the bow of the ship. Youthful exuberance and carefree abandon were personified in his monkey-like capers, and possibly no one

The Klondyke was popular vessel
(Herman Schnitzmeyer Photo)

had more fun than the small man himself — Jimmie Harbert.

The following is an ad which appeared in the Flathead Courier on July 8, 1915:

The 1915 registry of boats included the following:

Demersville	Mary Ann	New Klondyke
Dora	Albatross	Black Maria
Montana	Doman	Defiance
Kalispell	Skinkoots	Paul Bunyan
City of Polson	Betty C	Queen

and many others.

As lake transportation was much cheaper than land transportation, Jim Hill, agent for Great Northern at Somers, was handling most of the freight, and Nels Peterson, with Northern Pacific at Ravalli, received very little. This obviously presented a business opportunity, and an idea was conceived by men in Dixon and Missoula to operate a boat up the river from Dixon to a point near the Buffalo Rapids bridge, a distance of approximately twenty-five miles.

In the spring of 1912, The Dixon and Sloan Transportation Company was organized. Included on the board of directors were four Dixon men: Joseph Marcure, G. E. Whiteman, Harry Neffner, and Allen Sloan.

Select fir timbers for the boat were shipped from the Pacific coast, some of which were so large that they

76

required two flat cars to transport them over the rails. Built with a flat bottom, the boat was 80 feet long and had a 20 foot beam. When loaded to its capacity of 80 tons, it would draw only 15 inches of water — a vital necessity owing to the many rapids in the course of the river.

After one postponement, the launching was held at Dixon on September 21, 1912, with much pomp and ceremony. The Dixon band turned out in force to play appropriate music. Miss Chrissy Donlan, daughter of Senator Ed Donlan of Missoula, christened the structure "The City of Dixon," and broke a bottle of imported champagne over the bow. Ed Mulroney of Missoula was the major speaker at the launching. Captain D. M. Roberts, the skipper, wore a brilliant blue uniform, similar to those worn by fleet admirals. Amid the din of railroad whistles and cheering from the vast crowd, "The City of Dixon" slid into the water.

The launching of the craft was the only sucessful venture undertaken On its maiden voyage, the boat was unable to reach its destination due to difficulties in operation and treacherous river conditions. Believing that higher water conditions in the spring would improve matters, the owners docked the boat until 1913, and then "The City of Dixon" made one complete round-trip. By the fall of 1913, the company was in financial difficulties due to major expense and minor income.

Hopes for success were revived, however, in the following spring when Valley View farmers expressed an interest in supporting the water freight line with a shipment of hogs bound for the Spokane market.

On May 30, 1914, with "Cap" N A. Palmer at the wheel, "The City of Dixon" headed upriver with a load of freight for the Gus Norris' store at Norrisvale (now

77

known as the Buffalo Bridge), and a guarantee of a return load of hogs.

The boat got as far as Sloan's Ferry before trouble appeared in the form of a cable stretched across the river. The operator at Sloan's Ferry refused to let them through and bitter words ensued "The City of Dixon" returned to Dixon, an officer of the Law became a passenger, they returned to Sloan's Ferry, the cable was cut, and the boat went through, only to meet more difficulty in the rapids. In due process of time and trouble, they eventually reached Norrisvale and unloaded the cargo.

The Valley View hogs were loaded, and the boat headed downriver, stopping briefly at Sloan's Ferry for another load of hogs. After docking in Dixon, the running time was noted — eleven hours: nine hours to go upstream, and two hours for the return trip.

The Valley View farmers received a top price of 7c a pound for their hogs These men who had faith in "The City of Dixon" were C. M Peden, A. H. Hudson, Ira Afflerbaugh, G. H. Thompson, P. McMartin, C C. Phipps, and E. Boucher.

The trouble which brewed at Sloan's Ferry continued to simmer that summer and cancelled any further trips for the boat. Then fate took a hand and cancelled the high hopes of a progressive group of pioneers Fire completely destroyed "The City of Dixon."

The completion of the Northern Pacific railroad line into Polson in 1917, and the increased ownership and use of automobiles, greatly diminished revenues from both freight and passengers for the lake transportation companies. Financial conditions went from bad to worse for the navigation businesses. An effort was made by some of the Polson businessmen to keep the lake industry afloat, and in April, 1920, The Flathead Lake Company was organized. The incorporators were A. F. Mason, J. H. Cline, C A. Stone, W G. Dewey, F. L. Gray, William Irvine, J. L. McIntire, and Dr. G. B. Owen.

The newly-formed company bought all of the properties of the Hodge Navigation Company, the Polson-Somers Transportation Company, and the Flathead Navigation Company at a very reduced figure. The best boats were kept in service with the others scrapped for whatever could be realized from them.

Excursion trips were scheduled and rates reduced in an effort to attract the paying customer, but to no avail. The company could not compete with the newer and more modern modes of transportation. In September, 1925, the Flathead Lake Company went into the hands of a receivership. A year later, the city of Polson bought the company's dock and two warehouses for $1,000. And so marked the end of another colorful era on the reservation.

The history of Flathead Lake transportation would not be complete without more than a mention of Captain Eugene Hodge, Sr He gave forty-four years of service, although his career included some harrowing experiences, it was his proud and enviable record of never having lost a life on any boat he served.

Captain Hodge was born in Michigan in 1859. In 1872, he left home and began his life work on the water, working for several years on boats plying the Great Lakes Hearing of the building of the Great Northern Railway through Montana, he headed west in 1890

Captain Hodge was a big man, standing 6 ft 7 inches tall When he arrived at Ravalli, in May, 1890, he swung his pack on his shoulders and headed for the nearest body of water, the Flathead Lake. This tall man with the determined step attracted attention, not only from humans but from range cattle and buffalo. As he neared Ronan, a herd of buffalo came charging up to within a short distance of the hiker. Hodge stood still. With an abrupt motion, he threw his pack around his head. The startled buffalo scattered, leaving a relieved man and a trail of dust. He completed his journey, unmolested, and arrived at the foot of the lake

Being experienced in lake transportation, Captain Hodge had no trouble acquiring employment; he got a job on "The U. S Grant." He subsequently served "The Montana," "The Tom Carter," "The Mary Ann," "Kalispell," "Demersville," the original "Klondyke," and the "New Klondyke"

In 1924, although lake transportation appeared to be a thing of the past, Captain Hodge and his son, Frank, built a sturdy freighter at Big Fork He named the craft "The Jim Hill" in honor of his friend, the founder of the Great Northern Railway. Later he salvaged the top of the old boat, "The New Klondyke," and installed it on his freighter, which he re-named "The Klondyke"

Captain Hodge passed away in the home he loved so well — "The Klondyke" — on July 30, 1934

Three other men who were prominent and influential in the freight and passenger traffic on the lake were Ernest and Walter Von Euen and N. A. Palmer. These men were quite at home on a lake which could be calm and peaceful one moment and then suddenly turn into a fury of ten-foot waves

In this modern day and age, boats are still quite prominent on the Flathead Lake. Instead of carrying vital freight and passengers, the boats contain fishermen idling away a quiet hour or vacationers zipping across the water at top speed. As in all eras, a body of water continues to hold a fascination for mankind, and the Flathead Lake is certainly no exception.

Daydreaming on the Homestead — 1911. Bob Johnson
and his claim in Moiese area

Homesteading farm family on Flathead Reservation
(Photo by Flathead Irrigation Project)

CHAPTER TEN
Homesteading on the Reservation

In 1887, Congress passed the Dawes Act which included the provision that the Flathead Indian Reservation would be opened to white settlement, with the best lands to be allotted to the Indians and the surplus lands to be sold to homesteaders.

Major Peter Ronan, Indian agent, recommended that there be a delay in the procedure inasmuch as the Indians were not far enough advanced at that time to be thrown into intimate contact with the whites, and they were also opposed to being allotted.

Several years passed, and white men kept advancing westward, seeking new homes. Coming into the northwest, men found it to their liking, and many of them married into the tribes. More schools were established by the government and by the Jesuit priests at the Mission Major W H Smead, new Indian agent, and his sub-agents made good progress in advancing the culture of the Indians

On April 23, 1904, Congress passed a bill, signed by President Theodore Roosevelt, authorizing a survey to be made of the reservation lands and allotments to be made to the Indians Work was begun under the administration of a new Indian superintendent, Major Samuel Ballew, and the mammoth undertaking was completed in 1908

All of the lands on the reservation were classified. The Indians were allotted acreage that they had selected — many of them had previously made their choices and were living on them There was a total of 2,460 allotments made, in 80 acre and 160 acre selections Some of the Indians preferred the less desirable land, and were given 160 acre tracts Most of the Indian families were allotted land adjoining each other whenever possible

The five-man commission, which was appointed to classify the lands, found the following surplus lands available for homestead entry.

40,229 acres of agricultural land — 1st class — appraisal price, $7 per acre;

75,019 acres of agricultural land — 2nd class — appraisal price, $3 per acre;

336,189 acres of grazing land appraised at $1 25 to $1.50 per acre

In addition to the lands that were appraised for homestead entry, more than 60,000 acres were set aside for townsites, reservoirs, power sites, educational and religious functions and other special purposes. A large amount of acreage was reserved for anticipated births among the Indians. The total acreage of the Flathead Indian reservation was found to be 1,243,969

The settlement of the reservation was delayed a year due to the establishment of the Bison Reserve. With the sale of the Pablo buffalo herd to Canada, the U.S government realized that an effort should be made to preserve a vanishing herd

On May 22, 1909, President William H Taft issued the following proclamation, opening the Flathead lands to white settlement:

"All persons qualified to make homestead entry, may on and after the 15th of July, 1909, and prior to and including the 5th day of August, 1909, but not thereto or thereafter, present to James H Witten, Superintendent of the Opening, at the city of Coeur d'Alene in the State of Idaho, by ordinary mail, but not in person or by registered mail or otherwise, sealed envelopes containing their application for lands in the Reservation wanted, but no envelope shall contain more than one application and must be made out on forms furnished by the General

Land Office — applications for Flathead lands must be sworn to before a notary public at either Kalispell or Missoula, Montana."

The application form was as follows:

"I, ... of .... post office, aged .... years, height .... feet, weight .... pounds, in support of this, my application for registration for Flathead lands, do solemnly swear that I am a citizen of the United States, or have declared my intention to become such, that I am not the owner of more than 160 acres of land, and have not heretofore made any entry or acquired any title to public lands which disqualifies me from making homestead entry; that I honestly desire to enter public lands for my own personal use as a home and for settlement and cultivation, and not for speculation or in the interest of some other person; that I present this application for that purpose only, and have not presented and will not present any other affidavit of this kind

....

Applicant

The foregoing was subscribed and sworn to before me, after it was read to or by affiant, this .... day of ...., 1909

....

Notary Public"

Soldiers or sailors who were honorably discharged after ninety days' service during the War of the Rebellion, the Spanish-American War or the Philippine Insurrection did not need to apply at the registration points in person. They could register through agents appointed by them for that purpose, with power-of-attorney forms qualifying them to act

Persons not qualified to make homestead entry were:

1. A married woman, unless she has been deserted or abandoned by her husband, or unless her husband is incapacitated by disease or otherwise from earning support for his family, and she is the head and main support of the family.

2. One not a citizen of the United States and one who has not declared his intention to become such.

3 One under 21 years of age; one owning more than 160 acres of land or one who has used up his homestead rights prior hereto.

Anyone who had homesteaded on a unit of less than 160 acres could file for the remainder of a unit up to the total of 160 acres. As an example, if someone had proved-up on an 80 acre tract, he was entitled to file on a unit up to 80 acres

From July 10th until August 5th, in 1909, there were 81,363 people who registered for lands in the Flathead at Kalispell or Missoula When the applications reached Superintendent James H. Witten at Coeur d'Alene, they were thoroughly mixed in a large container and the envelopes were indiscriminately drawn one at a time, and numbered consecutively as drawn.

The first 3,000 so drawn names were then duly notified, the names were posted at the land offices in Kalispell and Missoula, and were also printed in the local papers

For homestead lands on the reservation situated in Flathead County and north of that line in Sanders Co., on May 2nd, the first fifty names were called at Kalispell; on May 3rd, the next fifty numbers were called and then one hundred names were called each day that week. The staff then went to the Missoula land office, where the same numbers were called in like manner for lands on the reservation located in Missoula County and that part of Sanders County lands on the reservation south of that line (The Missoula-Flathead boundary being the first section line running east and west just north of the Townsite of Pablo) This procedure continued alternately each week between the Kalispell and Missoula land offices at the rate of one hundred numbers each day, excepting Sundays, until 'all 3,000 names were called

Under the government terms, the homesteader had to pay one-third down of the appraised price at the time of selection of his homestead, and the balance in five equal annual installments The homesteader then had to establish residence on his land within six months Practically all lands were subject to irrigation construction charges by the U S Reclamation Service

Out of the 3,000 names drawn at Kalispell and Missoula, only 403 people selected homesteads and made the required down-payment The first name called was that of James Murray of Warsaw, Indiana, who failed to appear Joseph Lodge of Deer Lodge, Montana, failed to respond when his name was the second one drawn Patrick Quigley of Rosemont, Minnesota, whose name was called third, selected 160 acres near Big Arm and paid $1 25 an acre for it The ninth name drawn was that of Ralph R. Tower of Sisseton, South Dakota The next day he was on his selected homestead, located five miles northwest of Polson At the present time, Mr Tower is living on the same land

Others called, on that first day in Kalispell, included C L Brownell of Minnesota, B F Kashner of Seattle, Washington, L M Padgette of Creston, and Daniel E. Blair of Spokane All of these men made homestead selections across the river from Polson

In Missoula, on May 9, 1910, Edward M Weber of Hillyard, Washington, was the fourth name drawn, and the first to appear to make a selection He chose 80 acres which were located 1½ miles west of Ronan, with Mud Creek running through the corner of it. Mr. Weber had been a machinist in the Great Northern Railway shops at Hillyard Before filing for a homestead, he had gone over the reservation four times and believed he had found the best land offered. He was a bachelor, and stated that he was now looking for a lady partner who could shoot ducks and milk cows Lake county marriage records show that he found himself a partner, Anita Louise, but there is no mention of her marksmanship or milking ability. County records also show that on December 14, 1944, Edward Weber sold his 80 acres to Joe Piedalue of Ronan.

At the first drawing in Missoula, the following also took lands· Eleanor McClellan of Missoula, Alfred Wallin of Prairie Duchien, Wisconsin, Edgar S. Dorman of Missoula, H H. Goble of Great Falls, James R. Smock of Shenandoah, Iowa, D D. Miller of Grand Ronde, Oregon, Amandus Hinz of Spokane, Francis M Cammack of Seattle, Washington, D P. McIntyre of Eveleth, Minnesota, Harry Y Gephard of Missoula, Thomas C. Caswell of Missoula, Andrew Eck of Helena, Elizabeth Pfeiffer of Muscatine, Iowa, and John D Van Liew of Weldon, Iowa The widows of Messrs Goble and Smock live in St. Ignatius, Montana at the present time.

A large number of units for homestead entry remained after the first drawing; consequently on September 1, 1910, the holders of numbers 3,001 to 6,000 were called at the land offices in Kalispell and Missoula in the same manner as the first 3,000 Fred M. Murdick of Warsaw, Indiana, holder of number 3,055, selected a homestead in

Valley View on the first day of filing He lived on this unit until 1960, and now makes his home in Polson.

The number drawings in April and September did not exhaust the supply of homestead units available, and at midnight on October 31st, these remaining units were thrown open to the public, with squatter's rights prevailing The reservation teemed with activity and excitement as the hour of midnight approached The midnight run found doctors, lawyers, merchants, laborers . . . people from all walks of life . . . participating in this land-grabbing event. Some choice units had eight to ten people on them. There were no reported acts of violence, but the attorneys on the reservation were kept busy for some time to come, settling the squatters' difficulties

Two men and one woman met in the middle of a 40 acre tract about four miles northeast of Pablo, each wanting to lay claim to the land. After discussing the situation, the men left the land to the woman, Mrs. Maggie Crow, a widow Mrs. Crow and her son, Jesse, erected a tent and attempted to get a few hours of sleep before going to the land office the next morning to register their claim. Mrs. Crow proved-up on the forty acres in the prescribed time, and later married O. H. Peltier, who was the County Clerk and Recorder of Lake County from 1928 to 1936.

D. A. Dellwo of Charlo managed to get a homestead and a bride during the 1910 scramble for land. Most of the units were taken, and Mr. Dellwo laid claim to the same homestead that Mary Grace Caffidy had staked. He graciously let her file on it, and then married her. They are still living on that homestead. (D. A., however, postponed the wedding until after he also got himself a desirable homestead unit).

New Flathead Reservation residents arrive at Ravalli

(Photo by Flathead Irrigation Project)

Mission Valley welcomes new settlers at St. Ignatius

(F. I. I. S. Photo)

The land offices in Kalispell and Missoula opened at 9:00 A.M., on November 1st, and they did a brisk business as the homesteaders rushed to file their claims, each applicant falling in line as he arrived. James E. Hern made the fastest time recorded from the Polson area. At midnight, Jim squatted on his claim which was six miles southeast of Polson. He staked it down, then rode to Polson on horseback From there he boarded a fast motor boat to Somers, then went by auto to Kalispell. His total time was three hours and forty-six minutes. He proved-up on his homestead in due time, and lived on it for many years. Mr. Hern was the first Chief of Police of Polson.

The pilgrimage to the "promised land" of the Flathead in 1910, brought an influx of people from all walks of life and from all corners of the United States. Home-seekers arrived by train on the south at Arlee, Ravalli and Dixon; and on the north at Kalispell and Somers. The boats on Flathead Lake deposited many weary travelers at Dayton, Elmo, and Big Arm, but Polson received the major share.

Hotels and eating places were crowded to overflowing. People were living in log cabins, tents, and any available shelter. Carpenters and laborers were in great demand at $5.00 and $3.00 per day as business houses, dwellings, and buildings of all description were being erected as rapidly as possible.

There were seven banks operating on the reservation — one at Dayton, three at Polson, two at Ronan, and one at Dixon. But money was scarce. The rate of interest was 12% — paid in advance. If a pioneer borrowed $100, he received $88. The combined assets of all seven banks amounted to slightly over $300,000.

The first year for the settlers was a trying one. The summer was hot and very dry. Most of the people were living in hastily-built shacks that were hot in the summer and cold in the winter. Many of the farmers had to haul water from the nearest town or from available rivers and creeks.

Settlers, buffalo, range cattle, and wild horses met head on. The sudden invasion and general uproar created by the white people caused great unrest among the Indians. Their happy hunting ground was no longer happy, and was rapidly ceasing to be a hunting ground. Rumors flew that the Indians were planning to run the white people off the reservation.

The groundless rumors impressed two young homesteaders from the middle west. After spending a backbreaking day on their land about six miles south of Polson, they dropped into bed at night, completely exhausted. They were awakened in their one-room shack about midnight with the sound of howling coyotes. Thinking themselves surrounded by Indians intent on their scalps, the men barred the door and crawled under the bed. The real source of their terror — the coyotes — moved on to other ground, and the men sheepishly faced friends who kidded them unmercifully.

The dry and hot summer of 1910 was made more unbearable with the disastrous forest fires near Wallace, Idaho, which created a dense cover of smoke over the reservation. One of the stories to come out of this era concerns chickens. One Sunday in August, it became so dark at four o'clock due to the dense smoke, that all the chickens went to roost. It was a long night for them. The next morning, farmers on the reservation found eggs all over their chicken houses.

Not only the chickens were fooled. A guest at a small ranch five miles south of Polson — a man from Missouri — begged his host to keep a team of horses harnessed all night. He was sure the world was coming to an end, and when the fires got too close, he reasoned that they could at least have transportation to the lake, which might save them from a fiery death. He used the transportation the next day . . . to catch a train . . . and never came west again.

Many of the homesteading settlers were not bona fide tillers of the soil, being more at home in an office, a school room, or a store. Great dreams were shattered as some of the settlers realized they were square pegs in round holes, and they sold their rights for whatever the market would bear or left their homesteads outright with no remuneration other than calloused hands and aching backs. But the more hardy remained and bungled through and learned by experience, leaving a vast heritage for future

Schooling the many children on the reservation was quite a problem. Most of the Indian children attended their own schools at Ronan, the Jocko agency, or the St. Ignatius Mission, but for the youngsters of the white man it was a different story. There were no big yellow busses to transport the students to school, and due to the fact that there were families on every 80 or 160 acres, the schools were about four miles apart. In Irvine Flats, there were four two-room school houses with two teachers in each school. In Polson, during the school term of 1910-11, school was conducted in five different buildings, only one of which was owned by the school district. (This same frame building is still in service by the present-day district.) Similar conditions existed all over the reservation in regard to the elementary school level, and there was no high school level at this time.

The schools scattered throughout the farming areas were the gathering places for social or business meetings . . . the hearts of the small farming communities. The small pleasures the settlers allowed themselves, after many days of hard work, were enjoyed in the schools at country dances, box socials, etc.

The following will lightly illustrate the first year for a homesteading family.

The family of George Brown was excited. They were leaving Missouri to begin a new life in Montana. The six children were beside themselves with enthusiasm as they watched the family belongings being loaded on the emigrant train — a well-drilling machine, the household goods, two mules, two horses, a cow and calf, and some chickens. They waved to their father as he left with their possessions on March 30th.

On April 4th, Mrs. Brown and the youngsters boarded a home-seekers' train — destination: Ravalli, Montana. Traveling on the same train were ten men from the same Missouri locality. On April 7th, the home-seekers' train pulled in at Ravalli, just three hours behind the emigrant train which held the livelihoods of so many.

There were no accommodations available for the family, so the Brown family lived in a 12x14 tent at Ravalli for three weeks while Mr. Brown looked for some type of dwelling for them. Each night some of the furniture and household goods had to be moved outside so the family could go to bed, and each morning it was brought back into the tent. Mr. Brown found a house of sorts, and moved his family. It was a one-room log house, located on the open prairie in the middle of what is now the

Pablo Reservoir, with the distinction of having a dirt roof and a dirt floor. Mrs. Brown's main housekeeping problem was keeping the dirt floor clean.

After living under these crowded conditions for two months, the Brown family leased an 80 acre allotment five miles southeast of Polson. This was almost sheer luxury as the house, made of rough lumber, had two rooms in it and there was a water well close by.

On June 15th, twenty acres of freshly broken-up prairie were planted to oats. But the first year on the homestead was a dry one, and the discouraged family harvested two loads of oat hay, which included dirt, roots, and all.

Undaunted, the family dug in with determination. That winter George Brown and his oldest son kept the family sustained by sawing and selling wood. They purchased dry, standing trees from Dave Ashley at 25c a rick, sawed three ricks a day, and then hauled the wood to Polson where they sold or traded it, averaging $2.50 per rick.

The Brown children missed a year of schooling, but the family got through the winter, and when spring arrived, hope sprang eternal.

With perseverance and hard work, the George Brown family made a success of their life in Montana. Like others of their caliber, they remained on the reservation to become the pioneers and developers of greater things to come. The subsequent generations of these pioneer families can look back with pride, and look forward with hope.

"Brown" family is an alias. True name is McAlear.

Working on lower Crow Creek Dam, 1918, Flathead Irrigation Project   (F. I. I. S. Photo)

McDonald Lake spillway on Flathead Irrigation Project
(Herman Schnitzmeyer Photo)

Dry Fork Dam, Flathead Irrigation Project, near Lone Pine   (F. I. I. S. Photo)

CHAPTER ELEVEN
Irrigation — Development Unlimited

The key to the vast change that has taken place in the progress of the reservation since 1910 is irrigation.

The first irrigation on the reservation was done in 1855, at the St. Ignatius Mission. The Jesuit Fathers and their followers made ditches to move the water from the Mission Creek to the fields.

Encouraged and financed by the government, the first irrigation ditches in the Jocko Valley were built in 1872 for the Indians to aid them in producing better crops on their new homesites. The water came from the Jocko River and Finley Creek. An abundance of timothy hay and clover — natural crops for the reservation — were raised as well as grain, fruit, and vegetables.

Following this early development, individual Indians and white "squaw" men (so named because they married Indian women) constructed ditches from various streams on the reservation for the irrigation of their own crops, which grew profusely.

On April 23, 1904, Congress amended the homestead entry act to provide for the surveying and construction of works to irrigate the lands of the Indians and the lands acquired by the homesteaders. On July 8, 1907, a party was organized to make surveys and investigate the possibilities of irrigation on the reservation. The survey revealed the existence of at least 135,000 acres of land that were adaptable for irrigating. It was estimated that 78,000 acres could be irrigated by a gravity system, and 57,000 acres could be accommodated by pumping water from the Flathead River.

In 1908, under the regime of Project Engineer R. S. Stockton, the first $50,000 was appropriated to cover the

97

cost of surveys and beginning construction on an irrigation project. The first actual construction on the project was started in 1910, on the Jocko Unit, with an additional appropriation of $250,000 Sixty mules were purchased in Kansas City at an average cost of $250 each. Forty other mules and horses were transferred from the Shoshone Project in Wyoming. The construction equipment for these earlier irrigation projects consisted of plows, scrapers, fresnos, dump wagons, and smaller tools such as hammers, shovels, picks, bars, and carpenter tools. Most of the early structures were made of wood, which later had to be replaced with concrete The concrete for these gates and spillways was mixed by hand

In 1909, digging was started on the Newell Tunnel, named for engineer Willard Newell, who planned it, six miles below Polson The tunnel was to be dug 2,000 feet long for the diversion of the river so a power plant could be installed. The purpose of the plant was to pump water from the river to irrigate land which, it was believed, could not be irrigated by a gravity system. After two years of digging through rock with dynamite, pick and shovel, for a distance of 1,700 feet and a cost of $101,685.11, the tunnel project was abandoned when it was discovered that the land could be irrigated by a gravity system.

One of the largest contracts let on the Flathead project was made on September 14, 1911, to Nelson Rich of Prosser, Washington, for the construction of three dams and 8½ miles of canals. Of these dams — The Pablo, the North Pablo, and the Ninepipe — the North Pablo Dam had to be abandoned because it wouldn't hold water, it leaked through the hill into Polson. Nelson Rich had one of the major construction companies of his day. Two shifts a day operated most of the year round. Four mules, or horses, were hitched to the up-to-date dump wagons. The wagons were loaded with gravel and dirt with a steam shovel that was capable of keeping fifty wagons on the move, making the fills that constituted dams.

In 1912, a contract was let to the Wilson Brothers, Virgil and B. Joe, for the construction of ditches in Valley View. These ditches were built with mules, horses, picks, shovels, plows, scrapers, and fresnos.

In spite of these small beginnings, the path to an irrigated Flathead Reservation was long and dry. Appropriations from Congress were very meager; eastern Congressmen thought little of the west, and even less of Montana, and hesitated to allocate funds, believing they would never be repaid.

A dry cycle began in 1916, and the farmers and ranchers, who had been promised irrigation with their homesteads, put on a little heat themselves to get the desired action. Water users' associations were formed and the people bombarded their congressmen and senators with letters. The Polson Chamber of Commerce sent James Harbert, an ardent booster for irrigation, to Washington to see if the purse strings could be loosened. Later D A. Dellwo and others were sent to the national capitol to see responsible government officials.

By 1925, these efforts bore fruit. Congressman Louis C. Cramton of Michigan, Chairman of the Appropriations Committee for the Interior, made a trip to the Flathead to view the situation. He attended mass meetings of the water users, was filled with fried chicken and optimistic words, and returned to Washington to do what he could to see that the appropriations were forthcoming.

In 1927, moving slowly but surely, Congress asked that a repayment contract be set up, and this resulted in the formation of three irrigation districts The districts included the Jocko-Arlee unit; the Mission unit, south of Post Creek; and the Flathead unit, north of Post Creek and including Camas. There were twelve subdivisions which included Jocko, Revais, Mission, Ronan, Pablo, Round Butte, Valley View, Polson and Camas. These units contain a total of 142,096 acres of classified irrigable land on which more than 109,000 have now been placed under the irrigation project's maintenance and operation, and is being developed under irrigation

The commissioners of the Flathead Irrigation District revived the plan to develop the power plant that had been contemplated with the building of the Newell Tunnel, which was later abandoned. The proposed power plant would have a prime output of 7,500 horsepower

The plan drew angry protests from the Montana Power Company, which had made application through their subsidiary, Rocky Mountain Power Company, to construct a similar power plant on the same site, but on a much larger scale. The Montana Power Company strenuously objected to the government agency's plan for a 7,500 horsepower plant, and the opposition resulted in two years of bickering and dickering before an agreement was finally reached.

In 1928, Frank M. Kerr, president of the Montana Power Company, who had ridiculed the proposed "coffee mill" plant of the government, applied for a license which had to be approved by the Flathead Irrigation District. The District asked for a fifty-year lease which included 5,000 horsepower for pumping only, at 1 mill per kilowatt hour; 5,000 horsepower for project use or for sale at 1 mill per kilowatt hour; and another 5,000 horsepower for project use or for sale at 2½ mills per kilowatt hour.

100

When the Rocky Mountain Power Company applied to the Federal Power Commission for a license to develop the Newell site, in October, 1929, hearings were set in Washington, D. C., and were attended by two of the Flathead Irrigation District commissioners, A. B. Inkster and D. A Dellwo, and their attorney, Walter Pope. The hearings lasted two weeks, and the resulting lease to the Montana Power Company, through the Rocky Mountain Power Company, proved to be one of the richest blessings to ever occur in the history of the reservation.

The power company agreed to deliver power to the project in the quantity and at the low rates asked by the District. They agreed to pay the U.S. Government the sum of $101,685.11 for the use of the Newell Tunnel, and this sum was credited to the irrigation districts.

In addition, the power company agreed to erect a concrete dam at the site, approximately five miles downriver from the outlet of Flathead Lake;

To keep the level of Flathead Lake between 2883 and 2893 feet in altitude;

To complete all three units of power to generate 150,000 horsepower in three years;

To permit the U.S. Government to pump from the Flathead River, above the dam, 50,000 acre-feet of water for irrigation purposes after July 15th of any one year;

To pay the Tribal Council of the Confederated Salish and Kootenai Tribes, as rental for the use of the land at the site, a graduated scale starting at $60,000 the first year, and up to a maximum of $175,000 per year beginning the 20th year after the construction of the dam.

The Montana Power Company, however, was not allowed to sell power to private users on the reservation.

Their license was granted on May 23, 1930.

Since that date, no construction charges have ever been assessed against the irrigated lands. The operation and maintenance charges (approximately $3.50 per acre-foot of water), together with no assessment construction charges, makes the project one of the very lowest in the United States.

In 1938, the Flathead Irrigation District began the construction of a pumping plant two miles downstream from the Polson bridge, on the east bank of the river, in order to fulfill the needs of the project and comply with the terms of the lease.

The pumping plant contains three electrically-driven pumps with the pumping capacity of 67 cubic feet of water per second Each unit requires 3,000 horsepower of electrical energy for its operation. The pumps lift the water 335 feet from the river into a canal, which feeds it into other canals that route it to the Pablo Reservoir, or into the Polson B distribution system for irrigating the lands in the Polson district. The three pipe tubes from the river to the canal are four feet in diameter. Each pump is capable of moving 30,000 gallons per minute, or 138 acre-feet of water in twenty-four hours. (an acre 138 feet deep in water — by one pump in 24 hours).

On August 19, 1939, the first water was pumped into the new irrigation system. Lee Palmer, of Polson, has been the operator in charge of the pumping plant since 1940.

A pumping plant at Crow Creek has an electrically-driven pump with a capacity of 26 cubic feet per second, which requires 150 horsepower. It lifts the water 43 feet and diverts it to the Nine Pipe Reservoir or directly into the distribution system for the Charlo-D'Aste area.

The Revais Creek pumping plant, near Dixon, has a pumping capacity of nine cubic feet of water per second, requiring 100 horsepower. Lifting the water 79 feet from Revais Creek, it is then diverted into the Revais "R" canal for distribution in the Dixon area.

The Flathead Project, with headquarters in St. Ignatius, has shown steady growth through the years under the capable management of eleven project engineers. These engineers include R S. Stockton, E F. Tabor, F. T. Crowe, E. A Moritz, C J. Moody, H. Gerharz, G. L. Sperry, F. H. Brown, E L Decker, R. N. Parnell, and G. L. Moon.

The present irrigation system consists of fifteen reservoirs, with a total carrying capacity of 148,725 acre-feet of water. The largest dams retaining this vast storage of water are the Pablo, Nine Pipe, Crow, Hubbard, Mission, and McDonald Reservoirs.

There are approximately 1,300 miles of feeder and distribution canals and laterals, the largest of which is the feeder canal which collects the run-off water from the Mission Mountains and the canal outlet from the Pablo Reservoir. There are 150 major irrigation structures and 10,000 minor structures Some of the canals have been lined with concrete to prevent seepage, but there is still a certain amount of seepage from the Pablo Reservoir and its feeder canal which seeps through the hill and on north toward Polson.

The steady development of the reservation during the past few decades can be directly associated with the steady development of the irrigation project. Without irrigation, there would be no development unlimited — as it is today on the Flathead Project — yes, the Flathead Indian Reservation For this transformation, much credit is due three pioneer Commissioners of the Flathead Irrigation District, i e. A. B. Inkster, deceased, of Hot Springs; Charles Leavell, deceased, of Polson and D. A Dellwo, of Charlo. Credit is due many others, especially Ray Biggerstaff, who was the efficient secretary of the Mission Irrigation District from 1927 to 1953.

CHAPTER TWELVE
More Power To You

When the reservation was opened in 1910, there was a lot of horsepower but it was generated by four-legged creatures Electricity on the farms was unheard of, the homes being lighted with kerosene lamps and the yards illuminated with lanterns Power generated for the lighting of homes and businesses in the towns of the reservation was provided by steam or gasoline engines.

In Polson, the Northern Idaho-Montana Power Company operated a steam power plant which used wood for fuel This plant was in operation all day and up until twelve o'clock, when they shut it down until morning. A fifteen minute warning was given the residents that the "string would be pulled" at midnight. The rates charged were 20c per kilowatt hour for a residence, and 6c per kilowatt hour for commercial use The minimum monthly rate charged by the company for city-dwellers was $1.50 per month

As the reservation grew in population, the demand for power became more urgent and acute. This demand was magnified with the opening and operation of a flour mill, the first major industry to enter the reservation requiring electrical power for operation. When J H. Cline of Concordia, Kansas, began negotiations to open the mill in 1911, he was assured that there would be enough power to keep the mill in operation. But when the mill went into production in December, 1912, there was not enough electricity to operate all the equipment efficiently.

Power officials proposed that Cline put on a full night shift, and operate with limited services during the day Orders for flour had to be filled, however, and this necessitated around-the-clock operation of the mill.

105

F. F. Faucett, an engineer working for J H. Cline, located a stream of water, the Hellroaring Creek, five miles east of Polson. Hoping to use the water for a power plant, he filed a water-right on the stream and then discovered that Charles Allard, Jr had a prior right filed on the stream for irrigation purposes. Negotiating with Allard, Cline agreed to furnish the Allard ranch with electricity for twenty-five years in return for the right to use the water for the proposed power plant Then the Department of the Interior, Bureau of Indian Affairs, stepped in and claimed absolute rights to the water More negotiations, which included a trip to Washington, D C, for J. H Cline, produced the formation of the Mission Range Power Company and the granting of a lease for the use of the water. The officers of the company, organized in July, 1915, included J H. Cline, president; J. A. Johnson, vice-president, and C E. Wood of North Dakota, secretary and general manager.

The company immediately started construction on a dam for a water reservoir; the power plant, with its turbines and machinery, was located 588 feet below the dam. F F Faucett was the supervising engineer The Hellroaring Creek Power Project was completed on November 21, 1916, and the first electricity flowed through the newly constructed power lines into Polson.

The completion of the power plant brought about several changes affecting the reservation. The new plant developed 536 horsepower, which was more power than was needed by the flour mill, so the excess power was available for prospective users The Northern Idaho-Montana Power Company closed their steam power plant and sold their equipment and lines to the Mission Range Power Company Shortly thereafter new lines were

106

built to serve the towns of Ronan and Pablo. The rates for electricity were reduced to 12c for lighting purposes, and a 3c rate was charged to commercial users, for power and heating The minimum of $1.50 remained the same, and a 10% discount was allowed if the bill was paid by the 10th of the month.

Electric power was first developed on the reservation because a pioneer wanted to operate his business twenty-four hours a day.

In the summer of 1928, the Mission Range Power Company was sold to W. B. Foshay of Minneapolis, through his holding company, the Public Utilities Consolidated Corporation. The selling price was placed between $132,200.00 and $212,500.00, with the lower figure given for tax assessment purposes and the higher figure placed for electric rate-fixing purposes.

On January 22, 1929, the new power company lost one of its best customers when the Cline Flour Mill was completely destroyed by fire

During the years of 1929 and 1930, lines were extended to the towns of Charlo and St. Ignatius, bringing more light to the reservation. Charles Stanley was the general manager of the Public Utilities Consolidated Corporation.

Financial and electrical activity was stirring on several fronts at this time The Montana Power Company secured their license for the Newell Tunnel development through their subsidiary, The Rocky Mountain Power Company. Financial difficulties forced the Public Utilities Consolidated Corporation into the hands of a receivership. And during this era, the repayment contracts of the Flathead Project had been signed by the unit holders in the Mission, Flathead, and Jocko Irrigation Districts, promising them the benefit of economical electrical energy according to the terms of the lease signed by the Rocky Mountain Power Company.

All was not serene on the reservation; the defunct Public Utilities Consolidated Corporation and its patrons were at definite odds. The service was poor and some of the lines were deteriorating. On November 20, 1930, issues of The Flathead Courier and The Ronan Pioneer carried a message from D. A. Dellwo on behalf of the Flathead Irrigation District Commissioners, urging the government to purchase the properties from the Public Utilities Consolidated Corporation and extend the lines to serve all of the reservation, farms included.

And so it came to pass. On March 12, 1931, after months of negotiating, the Public Utilities Consolidated Corporation was sold to the Flathead Project, Bureau of Indian Affairs, for the sum of $160,000. Barry Dibble, consulting government engineer for the Bureau, was instrumental in the completion of the transaction Horace E. Bixby of Burley, Idaho, was the first power superintendent of the newly-acquired project properties on the reservation

The Hellroaring Creek plant, which was built in 1916, is as reliable today as in the days when it served the flour mill, and is still used continuously in the power system on the reservation

— Kerr Dam —

Construction of the Kerr Dam began as soon as the permit was granted on May 23, 1930, but operations were suspended on July 1, 1931, due to business conditions, and the Montana Power Company was granted an extension of time for its completion The contractors of the job, The Phoenix Utilities Company of Utah, resumed construction in July, 1936, with their contract calling for completion within three years. The building of the dam

108

Kerr Dam — Higher than Niagara!

(Montana Power Co. Photo)

proved to be a great boon to the economy of the reservation At the peak of construction, 1,200 men were employed. The huge project was completed a year ahead of schedule.

The Kerr Dam, located five miles below Polson on the Flathead River, is the largest electrical generating power plant in the Montana Power Company system with a total capacity of 180,000 kilowatts. The dam, which contains 85,000 cubic yards of concrete, is 204 feet high, 450 feet in length at the top and 100 feet in length at the base. The arch of the mammoth structure was designed for strength and is anchored deep in the rock cliffs on either side. The storage of water behind Kerr Dam, in the Flathead Lake, amounts to 1,217,000 acre-feet and is kept at an elevation between 2883 and 2893 feet above sea level.

The assessed valuation of the dam, from which Lake County receives 30%, is $9,656,714.00. The 1961 taxes totaled $406,413.75, which is 13.5% of the total tax load of Lake County. The total valuation of the properties owned by Montana Power Company on the reservation is approximately $30,000,000

The first unit of the Kerr Dam was completed in August, 1938, and residents of the valley didn't need a better excuse for a celebration. On August 6th and 7th, a festive mood hit the reservation as people came from far and near to attend the dedication and to enjoy the buffalo barbecue and the Indian War Dances. Kerr Dam was named in honor of Frank M. Kerr, the president of the Montana Power Company from 1933 to 1940.

The second unit of the plant was added in 1949, and the third unit was completed in 1954. With the 10,000 horsepower available to the Flathead Project upon completion of the dam, the rates to the users on the reservation under the irrigation projects were revised and reduced radically. Residential rates were 4c for the first 50 kilowatt hours, 2c for the next 50, and 1c for the next 900. For commercial users, the rates were as low as .8 of a cent per kilowatt hour In 1938, the total number of users was 2,482, and in 1961 that figure had jumped to 5,900. The total amount of power has more than quadrupled during that time, and the one major incentive for this increase, is one of the very lowest schedule of rates of any area in the State of Montana.

Although the major part of the reservation was well-lighted, one area had to content itself with kerosene lamps, gas lights, and lanterns The communities of Big Arm, Elmo, and Dayton were powerless due to the fact that they weren't in the irrigation districts. Their attempts to get electricity from Kalispell were fruitless because they were located on the reservation.

In 1947, Roy Proud and Mel Meuli of Dayton began intensive work in forming an REA (Rural Electrification Association) for the area. When the required number of members were secured and signed, in January of 1949, Mel Meuli and attorney Stanley Doyle of Polson made a trip to Washington, D C. to complete transactions, thinking the project was accomplished. But it required another trip in May, and the assistance of Senator Mike Mansfield, to secure approval of the contract between the Department of the Interior and the REA . . . a unique contract in itself inasmuch as it was between two governmental agencies.

In August, 1949, a sub-station was built near Elmo by the Cahill-Mooney Company. In November and December of that year, the lines were energized to all parts of the

Everbody celebrated at the dedication of Kerr Dam. This
picture was taken in the Kerr village below the dam on
dedication day.

district. New members were added, and the project proved to be a successful one. In 1958, the Indian Department took over the contract, paid off the remainder of the mortgage, and refunded the $10 membership fees to the 329 members. Since that time, this district has been a member and part of the whole Flathead Project, enjoying the same services and low rates as the rest of the reservation

During the past two decades, rapid expansion has taken place on the reservation, with the number of users of electrical energy greatly increased to include the farms, the rural areas, and the new industries such as the lumber and plywood mills. Power lines have been extended throughout the reservation, from the smallest home owner to the largest plant. The responsibility for this expansion has fallen on the shoulders of two capable men. A. V. Wynne was the Power Superintendent from 1940 until his retirement in 1955 — after nearly fifty years of work in the electrical field Al Sept, who took over the lines from Mr. Wynne, is the present Power Superintendent

The demand for current has greatly exceeded the supply on the reservation since the allotment of 10,000 horsepower was made in 1930 Additional power has been contracted for from the Montana Power Company. The Hellroaring Creek Power Plant, that once supplied the electrical energy for Ronan, Pablo, and Polson, could now only care for approximately 2% of the present demand for power.

The reservation has progressed from the earliest tallow candle in a log cabin to the present-day neons that light up the sky — and far-seeing pioneers made it all possible.

Early settlers, the M. A. Gilbert family, 1924
(F. I. I. S. Photo)

Here's an early day farm scene
(F. I. I. S. Photo)

114

CHAPTER THIRTEEN
The Land of Milk and Honey

Many of the homesteaders who arrived in 1910 were the first to sink a plow into the fertile virgin soil of the reservation Most of the land had never been cultivated, having been used primarily for grazing purposes, and the first crops of wheat, barley, and oats were bountiful. The irrigation system had not been developed at this time and all of the crops were derived from dry land farming. Wheat yielded 25 to 40 bushels per acre; barley, 50 to 60 bushels to the acre; and oats produced 60 to 100 bushels an acre.

The year of 1916 was a memorable one for many pioneers. On June 20th, snow began to fall in the evening, and by morning — on the first day of summer — there was at least eight inches of snow covering the reservation. At higher elevations, above Big Arm, the snow was ten to twelve inches deep, and many farmers went to town in sleds The snow stayed on the ground for two days, damaging fruit trees and telephone lines, but the resulting field crops were outstanding, with volunteer wheat yielding as high as 30 bushels to the acre.

And then came 1917. The United States entered World War I, and the reservation entered a dry cycle of years. Due to the crisis overseas, farmers were urged to plant a good acreage of wheat, and they did so, only to have it burned out by the hot sun and dry earth Those who were able to harvest their crops only realized 10 to 12 bushels per acre. During the following years there was a grave shortage of feed for livestock. In the winter of 1918-19, hay was shipped in from Minnesota and other out-of-state points Alfalfa hay, costing $48 to $50 per ton, was worth more than a two-year-old steer, but the ranchers paid the price rather than lose entire herds

The next decade saw conditions worsen — farm prices were low, interest rates were high, and although the need for irrigation was recognized, the plans were slow in formulating. With no immediate relief in sight, many farmers were selling-out and leaving for other locations.

The Northern Pacific Railway had a heavy investment in the reservation, and was concerned about the situation Their Agricultural Development Department, under the direction of John W. Haw of St. Paul, Minnesota, put on an extensive advertising campaign to interest settlers from the midwest and northwest in locating on the Flathead Project

The advertising aroused the necessary interest, and produced the need of experienced real estate men to secure listings of land on the Flathead Project, and to handle the homeseekers who were arriving. Mr. Haw and L. A. Campbell, the NP agricultural agent at Missoula, (now living near Skidoo Bay on Flathead Lake) located Bill and Pete Larsen who were successfully operating a land business in the Snake River Valley. The Larsen brothers opened their first office in Missoula, but in 1922 they moved to Charlo and occupied an obsolete Northern Pacific dining car and changed their firm name to The Great Western Land Company. As time went on, they moved to a vacant bank building in Charlo, and had a branch office in Polson

It took time and energy to get the necessary listings, and to find settlers who were financially able to buy, but in the latter part of the twenties, the Northern Pacific was sending special homeseekers' trains to the reservation. Volunteers with autos from the reservation communities met the homeseekers, and in conjunction with the Northern Pacific personnel, made tours over the project showing the farms and ranches. Free fish fries were held at Post Creek, and hot lunches were served in St. Ignatius and other towns. The homeseekers liked the fish, the farms, the scenery, and the hospitality, and the resulting negotiations were fruitful for all concerned.

The Northern Pacific, through the Great Western Land Company, brought in several carloads of dairy cows from the state of Washington These cattle were purchased on easy terms by the new settlers and by many who were already established By 1935, a census by the railroad showed that 732 farm families had been located, and of these there were 610 that were settled and well-rooted in the farm economy of the area. This was the beginning of a brighter era on the reservation — with water, cows, and alfalfa hay leading the way

Vast changes have taken place in farming methods and in the produced crops on the reservation during the past few decades In the area west of the Flathead River, and in the Irvine Flats, Garcon and Oliver Gulch sections, better methods of tilling the soil, and good summer fallow procedures have made the land more productive in the raising of dry land grasses and alfalfa. In the irrigation districts of Camas, Flathead, Mission and Jocko, the rotation of crops and the growing of a crop that is adapted to a particular soil produces such diversified crops as wheat, corn, oats and barley, timothy, blue grass, clover, Huntley mix and orchard grasses; alfalfa, potatoes, and sugar beets.

Agencies which have played a major role in the betterment of the lot of the reservation farmer are the Soil Conservation Service and the Farm Home Administration at Polson, and the County Agent at Ronan.

117

The County Agent, in conjunction with the Soil Conservation Service, has introduced scientific methods in the raising of crops on the project. These methods include the testing of soils, the application of fertilizer to correct deficiencies in each particular soil, the reclaiming of lands that need drainage, and the growing of better quality seeds. Sid Tietema, the Lake County Agent, has been instrumental in the improvement of farm conditions in the area

The Soil Conservation Service has heavy equipment for the leveling of land which is available to the farm operators at cost Officials in charge of the Soil Conservation Service are Nick Herak, Jr of Charlo, J. Ernest Lee of St Ignatius; Ralph Tower, George Thompson, and Cal Livingston of Polson. Specialists assisting out of the Polson office include Lewis Fuller, R G Lenz, Lloyd Fletcher, and Jack Cloninger

The Farm Home Administration, under the direction of R M Sherick, finances co-operating farmers who use the Soil Conservation Service facilities in the district.

Another agency which is helpful to the farmer is the Weed Control Agency, located in Ronan with H L. McIlroy, manager. This department will furnish machines for the spraying of crops, at cost, or will sell the spray ingredients if the farmer has his own spray rig

These services are under the Extension Service of the Montana State College and the U S. Department of Agriculture.

The following statistics are taken from the Montana Agricultural Statistics, issued by the Montana Department of Agriculture, co-operating with the U. S Department of Agriculture and the Agricultural Marketing Service of Helena, Montana The statistics quoted are

118

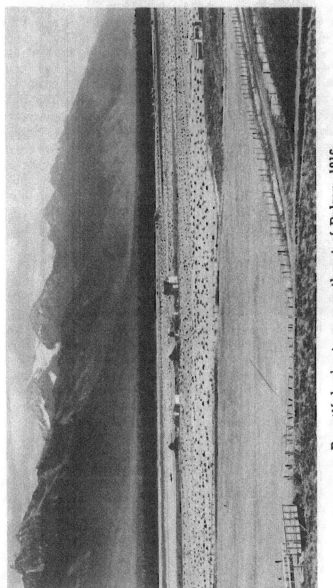

Bountiful wheat crop southeast of Polson, 1916

(Herman Schnitzmeyer Photo)

for Lake County Although there is a portion of the reservation lying in Sanders County, it is impossible to segregate the reservation figures from those of the rest of Sanders County

Year of 1959

Total value of all crops $2,396,500 00
Irrigated acres (listed) .... 49,860 acres
Non-Irrigated acres .... 53,570 acres

Crop	Acreage	Production	Value	Average Per Acre
Wheat, winter	15,700	431,600 bu	$703,500	27 5 bu.
Wheat, spring	7,500	170,700 bu	$273.100	22 8 bu.
Oats	7,300	315,800 bu	$202,100	43 3 bu
Barley	13,000	385,400 bu	$323,700	31 bu.
Hay, all kinds	56,900	97,200 tons	(one cut)	1 71 ton
Hay, alfalfa	40,300	75,000 tons	(one cut)	1 86 ton
Alfalfa seed	200	14,000 lbs	$ 4,200	701 lbs.
Corn	200	8,000 bu.	$ 10,400	40 bu.
Potatoes	790	142,200 bags	$492,000	300 bu
Sugar Beets	520	8,310 tons	$106,400	16 tons

One of the largest contributing factors in the development and advancement of farming methods is the mechanized equipment which is available for the use of the farmer In 1910, the breaking of the sod and "nigger wool" (a small, finely bladed grass with tough roots) was done with a "foot burner" — a one-furrow walking plow. Other machinery, such as riding gang plows, harrows, drills, binding machines and six-horse push binders, were powered by horses The threshing machines were motivated by steam engines A twenty-man crew was required to keep a big threshing machine operating at full capacity, in addition to the five men who operated the rig — which made a total of twenty-five men that had to be fed daily

120

Connerly Bros. combining in 1910 near Polson

by the women folk on the farm. Grain combines in the early days, powered by 26 head of horses, were not too successful owing to the heavy dew at night, loose soil in some areas, and the slow travel of the horses. These combines averaged 2½ miles per hour, so their demise from the farm scene was even faster when newer equipment was developed.

During the early years, wheat was sacked and hauled to Somers across the Flathead Lake on barges or hauled to Polson in wagons drawn by four or six horses.

The modern-day scene of the harvest is a different picture. The ground is prepared and seeded with machinery which is drawn by a tractor. The tractor will do more in three hours than four or five horses would do in nine hours. Today's mechanized threshing not only replaces the horses that were needed decades ago, but it

Combining today!

121

also replaces the crew of twenty-five men, and eliminates a lot of dishwashing for the women who had to feed them. Mechanized farming has enabled many of the reservation farmers to work an eight-hour shift at the mills in the Polson-Pablo area. They work from 4 p.m. until midnight in the mills, and use the daylight hours for farm work.

The majority of the grain raised today on the reservation is sold to Consolidated Dairies, Inc., who operates elevators at Polson, Pablo, Ronan, and Charlo, and to Teslow's, Inc, who has elevators and a mill at Ronan. K. Sagmiller is the manager of Teslow's.

— Sugar Beets —

The harvesting of sugar beets and potatoes, vital crops to the economy of the reservation, has undergone vast changes due to mechanization. Machinery is responsible for getting the sugar beets from the field to the refinery in Missoula where they are processed into sugar. The tops of the beets are cut off with a machine, another machine scalps what is left of the tops, a mechanized digger then lifts the beets out of the earth and they are placed on an elevator which moves them to another elevator. This elevator dumps the beets into boxes on a truck which follows the digger down the rows. The beets are transported to a railhead where they are elevated into open box cars, and thence on to the factory.

— Potatoes —

The favored specie of potato which is raised on the reservation is the Netted Gem. This crop has always grown to perfection, but for many years the market was unreliable — one year the farmers would receive good prices, and the next year they might have trouble even giving them away.

In 1937, two growers — D A. Hern and George Mangels, Sr. — planted certified Netted Gem seed in the Mountain View district. They interested growers from the state of Washington in purchasing the crop, to be used as seed, and thus opened a market for the Flathead Netted Gems. These potatoes are exceptionally clean and free from disease, and the demand for them as seed is good in the Yakima and Moses Lake valleys in Washington. Growers in the Pablo and Ronan areas raise about 800 acres each year to supply the demand.

The harvesting of this crop is fully mechanized. A machine is used to de-vine the tubers, then a digger lifts them onto a shaker. The smaller potatoes fall through the shaker onto the ground, and the larger ones are placed on the elevator which dumps them onto the bed of a moving truck. These potatoes are stored in potato warehouses during the winter, and in March they are sorted and sacked and shipped to the Washington areas.

— Horticulture —

In 1924, Stanley Scearce, Sr of Ronan, an early-day reservation booster, selected a name for the area from a large list submitted by residents. His choice, "The Garden of the Rockies," was very applicable. The reservation is not only bountiful, but versatile. Apples seem to thrive on the growing conditions. Yellow and red Delicious apples are grown for commercial use; other species which are prolific are McIntosh, Wealthies, Ben Davis, Yellow Transparent, and Crab Apples. Plums, pears, strawberries, sour cherries, and a wide variety of small berries do equally as well. Wild plums grow in profusion in the Dixon area, and wild huckleberries entice pickers into the woods with mouth-watering visions of pies and jams.

123

Garden vegetables grow in such abundance that many growers are unable to dispose of their crops

One fruit which has been developed, and always finds a ready market, is the Flathead sweet cherry This popular fruit hits the market after the Washington sweet cherries have been harvested, and due to the superiority in color. firmness, and size, the Flathead sweet cherry demands a premium price. Carloads of the fruit are shipped to points in the east, such as New York, and a market is also available in the Chicago area

In the spring of 1930, eight men pioneered the cherry industry when they planted several hundred Lambert sweet cherries and a sufficient number of pollenizers, the Black Tartarians The trees were planted on the hills east of Polson, along the east shore of the Flathead Lake, and around Skidoo Bay by Andy Connolly, Billy Lane, Dr J. L Richards, A E Williamson, Charles Mullen, Stanley Thurston, H A Johnson, and E E Mac-Gilvra

The trees grew well, and hopes were high, but in the winter of 1936, every tree winter-killed The growers came right back and replanted every tree that spring. The trees grew, waxed strong, and bore fruit prolifically. Since that time, many growers have been added to the list of sweet cherry raisers In addition to Lamberts, some Bing cherries are grown The pollenizer varieties used are the Van, Deacon, Starks, Gold, Centennial, Black Republican, and the Black Tartarian. Different varieties of pollenizers are used as they bloom at varying times. thereby giving the Lamberts and Bings a more even distribution of pollen Too much pollen at one time produces a smaller cherry The pollenizers are sold primarily for maraschino, dipping chocolates, and cocktail cherries.

124

Approximately 600 acres of sweet cherry trees are grown in the Flathead Lake area, with 450 acres on the east shore and 150 acres on the south shore. It is estimated that one-half of this acreage is located on the reservation.

There are two marketing organizations for the sweet cherries grown in the area: The Flathead Lake Cherry Growers, Inc, at Kalispell and the Flathead Sweet Cherries Association at Polson Officers of the association are Stanley Thurston, president, E. C. Carpenter, vice-president; and A C Hoefert, secretary. Both organizations work jointly in the marketing of the fruit, with 80% marketed through the Kalispell plant, and 20% through the Polson plant During the latter part of July, when the packing season is at its peak, 150 people are employed at the Polson plant and warehouse, and 400 people are employed in the orchards

The average price received by the grower is 22.59 cents With the average expense to the grower amounting to approximately 6c, the economy of the area receives a real stimulus in the amount of about $250,000.

— Apiary —

Long before the white man arrived on the reservation — even before it was designated a reservation — the Flathead area was known as the land of milk and honey, with accent on the honey. On the east shore of the lake, above Yellow Bay, a bear went in search of something for his sweet-tooth. He found a tree loaded with honey. Ignoring the few bees that buzzed around, he robbed the comb and soon found that there were more than a few bees buzzing around As he swatted and danced and dodged, several Indians arrived on the scene and were regaled by his painful antics They promptly named the place The

Bear Dance Ranch, and so it is known to this day. A ranch in the area is named The Honey Ranch.

Since the opening of the reservation, it has become a haven for honey bees. The planting of clovers and alfalfa seemed to insure a home for the bees. It is estimated that during the 30's and 40's, there were at least 10,000 colonies of bees and the yield per hive averaged about 100 pounds of honey

Although modern methods of farming have improved the growth of crops, they have taken their toll in another field — the honey bee. Spraying for the control of insects detrimental to crops has decreased the bee population. Today there are about 5,500 colonies of bees, with the average yield per hive running around 70 pounds. The honey tradition is still being carried on by six bee-keepers on the reservation: J. F. Meade of Pablo, Leo Basler of Polson, K. W. Morgan of Hot Springs, T. J. Rowe of Arlee, and J. D. Harrah and Charles Scott of Ronan

The market for Flathead honey has generally been a good one, but during the past year, competition from South America has lowered the price 3c per pound. The South American honey is not as good in color or flavor, but California honey-buyers mix it with the Montana honey to get a better quality. Honey can be produced cheaper in South America than in the Flathead, and the high-quality Montana honey has to suffer the consequences.

If the demand for Montana honey continues to lessen, due to an imported cheaper product, the land of "milk and honey" won't be concerned about the milk, but the honey will be in jeopardy.

— Livestock —

The past fifty years have brought forth many changes in agriculture, and the raising of livestock is no exception. Pioneer cattlemen sent their steers to market when they were four or five years old, and the cattleman of today seldom holds his beef beyond two years. Modern methods of range control and feeding send better beef to the butcher. The advanced science of veterinary medicine is a small insurance to the stockman that the mortality rate of his herd will be lower than that of his predecessor's.

Homesteaders arriving on the reservation in 1910 imported all types of cattle, many of which were a mixture of beef and dairy breeds. These earlier cattle did not command good prices when they hit the market, and eventually the herds improved with better breeding policies.

During the 1920's, when a new group of settlers arrived, there was an interest in the better grades of dairy and beef cattle. Farmers and ranchers discovered it was easier and more economical to raise a good grade of cattle than it was to put time and money into a "scrub." Dairy cows were shipped in from Wisconsin and Washington, and better beef cattle were purchased with pure-bred sires.

Today there are many breeders of pure-bred cattle on the reservation. While the Hereford breed, both polled and horned, is the predominating beef herd, the Aberdeen Angus is coming ahead in popularity, and the Shorthorn cattle also meet with favor. Feed lots, where the cattle are "finished" with grain feeding, are coming more and more to the front in the cattle industry The cattle are marketed as short two-year-olds, weighing between 800 and 1,000 pounds Most of the cattle from the reservation are marketed at the Missoula Livestock yards, with top prices for steers ranging from 22c to 25c and cows bringing 14c to 16c

According to statistics released by the State Department of Agriculture in Helena, in 1960, 45,400 head of beef cattle were sold, and 8,500 head of dairy cows were sold out of Lake County, with a total valuation of $4,254,578 00

The dairy industry has shown the greatest evolution during the past thirty years In many cases, the early-day farmer milked his milch cows outside in the barn yard, squatting on his heels or sitting on a bucket or stool Quite often, the cows were fed no grain yet were expected to produce their fair share of milk And the breed of cow? Well   she was just a cow.

Today, the dairy cow is predominantly a good grade Holstein, Guernsey or Jersey The dairy cow is put into a milking parlor which generally has hot and cold running water. She is fed grain, washed thoroughly, and milked with a machine which has lacteal fluid pumped into the tubes Human hands never touch the milk which flows from the milking machine into a stainless steel enclosed tank When the creamery truck arrives, the milk is pumped from the tank into another sterilized tank on the truck The milk is transported to the creamery where it is homogenized or pasteurized, and then packaged in waxed cardboard containers for retail sales

The total income received by dairymen of Lake County for milk produced in 1961 approximates $1,840,-000 'Figures furnished by the County Agent's office and by Consolidated Dairies of Lake County show the purchase price paid to dairymen by three major creameries:

Community Creamery of Missoula $1,125,000
Gold Medal Dairies — processing at Stev-
   ensville .... $ 210,000
Consolidated Dairies of Lake County, at
   Ronan ... . $ 455,325
* Figures which cover that part of the reservation which lies in Sanders
  County are not available

The Consolidated Dairies of Lake County was incorporated in 1943 Their processing plant, located one-
half mile south of Ronan, was built at a total cost of
$318,605, which includes the garage and heating facilities.
Dairy products which are produced in this plant include
cream, butter, cottage cheese, ice cream, and cheddar
cheese. The corporation has 740 members, and the officers
are: William Evans of Charlo, president, John Boller of
St Ignatius, vice-president, M E Priest of Pablo, secretary; Floyd R. Olson of Ronan, manager, and Al Lillethun
of Ronan, elevator manager.

Agriculture, a major industry on the reservation, has
kept pace with the changing times, and the land of milk
and honey remains "the garden of the Rockies."

Andrew Nelson and George Laniger got a big one near
Dayton!

Tom Meuli and Federal Logging truck, 1921

CHAPTER FOURTEEN
The Lumber Industry

The Flathead Indian Reservation was blessed by nature with forests of big fir, larch, and ponderosa pine trees. Down through the years, these trees have warmed the hearths and brightened the economy of many men.

The first sawmill on the reservation was built by the Jesuit Fathers at St. Ignatius in 1856. It was a crude affair made of wagon wheels, a circle saw, and a carriage, but it served the purpose.

In 1861, a more modern mill was erected by the U.S. government at the Jocko Agency near Arlee for use by the Indians. In the 1890's another government sawmill was built near Ronan.

The first privately-owned sawmills were installed around 1904. Ben Cramer, who had married into the Flathead tribe when he wed Clerency Ducharme, operated a sawmill on the lake near Polson — just west of the present-day Country Club His brother, W M "Bill" Cramer, joined him in the business in 1909, and it became known as the Cramer Bros. Lumber Company. The Dupuis brothers, Caville and Victor, processed logs at their mill eight miles southeast of Polson, near the foothills of the Mission Mountains.

With the opening of the reservation to homesteaders, the demand for lumber increased. There were five lumber yards in Polson which were supplied with lumber, by way of barges on the lake, from the W. G. Dewey mill near Rollins. In the latter part of 1910, Dewey opened his own lumber yard in Polson with L L Marsh as manager.

Business was good for the lumber companies and mills as towns and farms were being built all over the reservation The mills turned out 15,000 board-feet of

131

lumber during a nine-hour shift, and most of the homes built in the areas of Polson, Ronan, St Ignatius, and Hot Springs were made of the best of the rough pine boards which sold at $15 per thousand feet

In 1912, W. G Dewey and Charles Glattly leased the Cramer Bros Lumber Company They later bought it outright, moved it to a site adjoining the City of Polson, and named it the Dewey Lumber Company This mill and lumber yard operated until 1943 when it was sold to the Polson Lumber Company

Some of the mills in operation during the early era were Pitts of Hot Springs and Ravalli, Niles of Ronan; Henderson of Pablo, Papenfuss of St Ignatius, and The Dupuis Brothers

The small mill is now a thing of the past with possibly one or two exceptions Higher stumpage for logs, longer hauls, improved machinery and big mill competition, together with fires that have destroyed so many mills, have combined to bring about the demise of the smaller mill. The Dupuis Bros Lumber Company, southeast of Polson, is one of the few remaining, but the continued growth and advancement of this mill took it out of the smaller class

The northern quarter of the reservation supports five mills, one of which operates two shifts per forty-hour week These mills are the Tom Wheeler Mill near Pablo, the Plum Creek Lumber Company, Inc, plant No. 2, also at Pablo, The Danielson Brothers Lumber Company, north of Pablo, The Dupuis Brothers Lumber Company, Inc, southeast of Polson; and the Marshall James Lumber Company, Inc, in Polson.

— The Tom Wheeler Mill —

Tom Wheeler is a veteran sawmill man, having been in business since 1924 when he opened his first sawmill at St Mary's Lake near St Ignatius He continued this operation until 1957 when he moved the mill north of Pablo to a site adjoining the Plum Creek Lumber Company.

Timber is purchased on the reservation, and the timber operations are conducted by the Pierce Logging Company of St Ignatius. The logs are run through a circular-type saw and cut into railroad ties, also sixteen-foot logs are sawed into lumber. The Plum Creek Lumber Company markets the output of this mill The mill operation is a family affair, with Tom Wheeler employing his sons and sons-in-law The five men have an output of 10,000 to 12,-000 board-feet per shift

— The Danielson Bros. Sawmill —

The Danielson Brothers Sawmill, located just north of the Plum Creek Lumber Company, plant No 2, began operation in January of 1959 They employ ten men and have an output of 40,000 to 50,000 board-feet per eight-hour shift Known as a stud mill, the output includes railroad ties and eight-foot length studding for building construction The entire production of the company is marketed by the Plum Creek plant The mill is operated by electric power, with most of the logs derived from reservation timbers

— The James Lumber Company, Inc —

The newest lumber company on the reservation, The James Lumber Company, is located adjacent to the U S. Plywood plant in Polson Officers of the company include Marshall S James of Polson, president, Rodney Witt of Whitefish, vice-president, and Herb Peschel of Whitefish, secretary-treasurer The plant employs nineteen men with an output of 55,000 board-feet per shift

The eight-foot logs which are put through this mill begin their journey at the circular saws The larger logs are sawed by two circle saws, one above the other, and the small logs and cores are sawed by two smaller saws operating side by side. The resulting lumber from each set of saws is then put through a rip saw, converting it into 2x4 studs The lumber is then taken off the green-chain, piled, and taken by lumber-lift tractors into the yard for a drying period. When the lumber is dry, it is run through a planer then graded, loaded and shipped to market points east of the Mississippi.

— The Dupuis Bros. Lumber Company —

Ed and Pete Dupuis, native sons of the reservation, began their sawmill careers in 1934 when they set up their first sawmill eight miles southeast of Polson. The demand for lumber was good, due to the construction of the Kerr Dam, but the operation of the mill was on a small scale with an output of 20,000 to 25,000 board-feet per day. This was run through a circular saw rig which was powered by a threshing machine engine.

In the early 1940's, the timber supply in the Polson-Ronan area was almost depleted, so the Dupuis brothers moved their mill to Dog Lake, between Hot Springs and Plains. The timber supply was abundant, and the mill improved to such an extent that it raised the output to 50,000 board-feet per shift. As the operations at Dog Lake increased, Pete's son, Oliver, and Ed's son, Lyle, joined the company.

Each year the stands of available timber grew more distant from the mill, and transportation costs were eating into the profits. In the fall of 1958, the firm decided to locate on a site two miles southeast of Polson, and construction was begun on a modern mill by the Rolfson Construction Company The plant building was made of a steel framework covered with corrugated galvanized

Dupuis Brothers Lumber Co., near Polson, 1962
(Meiers Studio Photo)

Plum Creek Lumber Co., Pablo division, 1962
(Meiers Studio Photo)

**U. S. Plywood Corp. plant at Polson, 1962. In foreground
is James Lumber Co.'s mill**
(Meiers Studio Photo)

sheeting The operation at Dog Lake closed down in the fall of 1959, and the new mill roared into action in the early spring of 1960

The Dupuis Bros Lumber Company employs thirty men at the mill, which operates one shift a day There are twenty-five men on the payroll who work in the woods During the hauling season, eight to ten trucks are kept moving with their loads of logs The output of the mill is 100,000 board-feet per 8 hour shift

In 1762, a small ponderosa pine seedling sprouted in what is now known as the Bassoo Peak area, forty miles northwest of Polson By the time the tree reached the age of two hundred years, it measured four feet in diameter and was one hundred feet tall It was one of many pine trees in the area controlled by the Flathead Tribal Council, and the stand of trees was sold to the Dupuis Brothers This area is sixteen miles from the highway at Niarada — eight miles of which is county road, and the remaining eight miles were constructed by the logging company

One day in June of 1962, a skilled lumberjack felled the big pine with a power chain saw The limbs were removed with a chain saw, and the tree was cut into 32-foot lengths When the chain-saw crew moved on to other trees, a D-7 tractor moved in and skidded the mammoth pine sections a quarter of a mile to the logging road where they were decked Waiting for a load was a 72,000-pound-capacity International truck and trailer This outfit, which cost $30,000, weighed 30,000 pounds, and rolled on eighteen tires

A Heil Boom tractor, with a crane lift and powerful grab-hooks, lifted the 32-foot logs, one at a time, and placed them on the logging truck, making a full load which would eventually produce 6,000 to 7,000 board-feet of lumber The truck driver chained the load securely, put his truck in gear, and headed for the Dupuis Mill, arriving there in 1½ hours.

At the mill, the truck driver released the chains and binders, and a tractor with a power lumber-lift pushed the pine logs off the truck and lifted them to a trough conveyor entering the mill. The logs first encountered a debarker which chewed the bark off and sent it on a conveyor to a burner. Then a chipper chewed on the outside of the logs, and the chips were power-blown through a pipe into a gondola car on the railroad track.

An operator in a small cage pushed a button that eased the pine logs into the mill to the saws. When the ponderosa pine was half-way into the mill, opposite a power chain saw, the operator pressed an electric button and the chain saw descended, cutting the log in half. Moving along the conveyor, one sixteen-foot section moved to the right and one section moved to the left, headed for the carriages on either side. The logs were banged onto the carriages by the sawyer and automatically pinned down. One-inch boards were sawed off the logs as they passed a seven-inch band saw. These one-inch boards were carried by an off-bearer to a rip saw, where they were ripped to the best sizes, then they were conveyed to trimmer saws and on to the green chain.

The lumber was taken into the yard by tractor and stack-piled to dry. When it was dry, the lumber went through the planer, which is capable of planing 7,000 feet of rough boards in less than fifty minutes. The shavings from the planer were blown through a pipe into a burner one hundred feet away.

The chips from this log, and others, which went into the gondola railway car, were shipped to the paper mill near Missoula The average output of these chips, which were originally burned as waste, is 1½ carloads per day.

The ponderosa pine, with its small beginning in 1762, eventually was shipped somewhere west of the Mississippi, and a small part of Montana became a home for a farmer on the midwestern plains

— Plum Creek Lumber Company, Inc., Plant No. 2 —

In April, 1958, the Plum Creek Lumber Company of Columbia Falls purchased 137 acres of land one mile north of Pablo, and soon thereafter construction was started on a large planing mill Later a complete sawmill unit was built Officers of the Plum Creek Lumber Company are D C. Dunham, president, L O Rude, general manager, and Jack Christofferson, plant manager of plant No. 2.

One hundred and forty men are employed to fill the two shifts that operate the plant, and seventy-five men are employed in the woods The average production for the mill is 90,000 board-feet of lumber per shift. The average output of chips for both shifts is four carloads, which are shipped to the Waldorf Paper Company in Missoula.

The main source of the mill's timber supply is in the Swan River Valley, which lies fifteen miles east of the plant, but due to the routing of the roads it necessitates

138

a seventy-five mile drive. The logging operations are handled by the Royal Logging Company of Columbia Falls which keeps 35 to 40 big trucks rolling.

The better grades of lumber are kiln-dried. The two kilns, which are 60x80 feet, have a capacity of 180,000 board feet The average drying time is 70 hours. Most of the lumber is shipped east of the Mississippi, from Florida to New York. Some railroad ties are sold to the Northern Pacific Railway. During the year 1961, approximately 46 million board-feet of lumber were processed in this mill.

— The Plywood Plant —

Leo Sensabaugh was a man with an eye to the future. Having been an employee of the United States Plywood Corporation in Seattle, when he later bought an interest in the Polson Lumber Company and settled on the reservation, he recognized a future for a plywood mill in the area. He hoped to make veneer plywood from the fir and larch timber that grew abundantly on the reservation.

On June 8, 1951, Leo's dreams began to materialize when articles of incorporation of the Polson Plywood Company were recorded by the Lake County Clerk and Recorder The document showed the authorization of capital stock to be issued — 200,000 shares at $1.00 per share. It further showed that five shares of stock were issued to the directors: Leo Sensabaugh, Mary A. Sensabaugh, A. L Helmer, Ruth C Helmer, and Lyle Manning.

In the summer of 1952, the Polson Plywood Company leased a small piece of lake shore property from the Polson Lumber Company. A shed was erected on this -site, which was just west of the lumber company, and a second-hand Capitol slicer from the U. S. Plywood Corporation was installed. A few pieces of vertical-grain larch and fir were processed, and a sales campaign was begun by Mr. Sensabaugh who used the veneer samples in his demonstrations.

On March 10, 1953, officers were elected for the corporation, and they were Leo Sensabaugh, president; William Pound, vice-president; Lyle L. Manning, secretary; Harry O Smith, treasurer; and J. H. Hanson, director. A campaign for the sale of stock was intensified, and in February, 1954, contractors were asked to submit bids for the erection of buildings The contract for the construction of buildings for the first plywood mill in the state of Montana was awarded to Merritt Cass & Sons of Polson on March 14, 1954. The contract specified that the work was to be completed in ninety days. On March 20, 1954, Governor Aronson turned the first shovel of dirt in the ground-breaking ceremonies for the erection of the first plant of its type in the state.

The buildings were completed within the specified time, equipment was installed, and the mill began operation with the first sheets of veneer rolling off the lathe by the middle of September. The sheets of veneer were cut, bundled, and shipped to points in the northwest. The Polson Plywood Company was in business.

A total of fifteen men were employed in the mill and in the woods. That fall and winter, new machinery was added and the kinks were ironed-out of the production line A New Coe Section 4 line dryer was installed, as was a Globe Glue Spreader, and the first carload of sheeting plywood was shipped on May 13, 1955.

From that time forward, the record of the Polson Plywood Company was one of progress New machinery was added, new and improved tractor lumber-lifts were bought, new buildings were constructed, and better footing was made for the machinery. The production of the plant was two million board-feet of ⅜ inch plywood per month. The success of the company seemed assured. The products were marketed by Larchmont Sales Company of Portland, Oregon. This sales contract was later sold to Mackie & Lewis of Seattle.

Will Tiddy was named general manager of the company in 1957, and it was under his management that the business continued to flourish. Being the only plywood company in the state, outside interests were attracted by the operation and the quality of the plywood produced. During the summer of 1959, Charles W Fox, president of Cascades Plywood Corporation of Portland, Oregon, began negotiations to purchase the Polson Plywood Company After some deliberation, the stockholders voted to accept the offer.

Under the ownership of Cascades Plywood Corporation, new buildings and equipment were added Improved machinery was installed, and the production was doubled — from two million to four million board-feet of ⅜ inch plywood per month. Two and a half carloads of chips per day were shipped to the Waldorf-Hoerner Paper Products Company of Missoula for paper manufacture

In January of 1962, the United States Plywood Corporation became interested in the local plant, and on February 23, 1962, a merger of the Cascades Plywood Corporation with the U S Plywood Corporation was completed. The U S Plywood Corporation is the largest plywood operation in the world Gene C Brewer of New York City is the president of the corporation, Marshall R. Leeper is a director and vice-president of the west coast operations, Charles W Fox is the vice-president of the Cascades Division and the Oregon operations of the corporation. Will Tiddy is still the manager of the Polson plant.

A tour of the plant at Polson shows the processes involved from the log to the finished product.

Logs, thirty-four feet in length, are brought to the mill yard by logging truck and rail where they are scaled separately into peelable and sawmill logs. They are then placed on the log deck where they are cut into eight-foot blocks. The logs are barked on a Globe scraper head barker, then transported by fork lift to the steam vats where they are steamed from four to sixteen hours. Taken from the vats, they are loaded onto an Ederer charger which charges the Coe lathe, peeling the blocks to a thickness of 1/4, 1/8, or 3/16 veneer. This operation peels the block down to a seven-inch core. A block 3 feet in diameter will peel approximately 300 lineal feet of ⅛ inch veneer.

The veneer travels over a series of trays to an automatic clipper which clips out the defects and cuts the veneer into widths of 27 and 54 inches. The veneer is then fed through two dryers, taking fifteen minutes for the process. After the veneer is dried, it is graded and laid up into panels of various thicknesses at the spreaders. The Polson operation has two spreaders with five men on each spreader on a three-shift basis. After the panels are laid and glued at the spreaders they go into an Ederer press where they remain under designated pressure for a period of approximately eighteen minutes. From the press, the panels go to a curing department for at least four hours. They are then cut into four-foot widths and eight-foot lengths The Polson mill also has a sanding department where the panels are brought up to grade by a series of patching operations and then run through an eight drum Yates sander. The stock is then ready for shipment throughout the nation.

At the present time there are 130 men employed at the Polson plant, with an annual payroll exceeding ½ million dollars. The plant is a member of the Douglas Fir Plywood Association which is a testing agency that assures the consumer of a quality panel that meets definite grade standards.

Timber for this modern-day operation is secured by bid from the Northern Pacific Railway, state, federal, Indian, and privately-owned timber stands. The logging and hauling, other than that brought in by rail, is handled by the Claridge Logging Company of Polson.

— Christmas Trees —

The reservation Christmas tree business was pioneered in 1932 by J. J. Thomas, ably assisted by Mrs. Thomas, when a yard was opened in Dayton. Mr. and Mrs Thomas are still in the Christmas tree business, and presently have a yard in Polson.

This seasonal business, which lasts during the months of October and November, has attracted many more participants. To date, there are yards in Hot Springs, Niarada, Dayton, Elmo, Polson, Ronan, St. Ignatius, Ravalli, and Arlee The average total output per year is 150,000 bales of trees . . . each bale contains an average of five trees. The trees are shipped to the midwest and the south In 1961, a carload of reservation Christmas trees were sent to Mexico.

The source of supply for the traditional tree comes from the tribal lands on the reservation, bringing in approximately $75,000 annually to the tribes. The trees are systematically cut for forest preservation under the

143

direction of Paul Clements, Supervisor of Forests, and Joe Jackson, Forester, both of the Agency at Dixon.

The Christmas tree business gives employment to 100 people in the yards and 200 workers in the forests, which brings Christmas cheer in more than one way.

The versatile lumber industry plays a vital role in the economy of the reservation. Pioneered by settlers needing shelter, the reservation timber today provides beauty and warmth for homes all over the nation.

Bob Johnson mill near Ronan, country style 1930

Logging, 1962 style, by Claridge Logging Co., Polson
(Flathead Courier Photo)

144

CHAPTER FIFTEEN
The Skyways of the Flathead

In the earlier days of the reservation, only birds filled the skyways of the Flathead Although man had long-dreamed of travel through the air, he left the actual flight to his feathered friends and contented himself with transportation on land and water

The first flight of a machine through the skies above the Flathead occurred on July 27, 1913, when Terah T Maroney made the first take-off and landing from water in the northwest, using the Flathead Lake for his landing strip. The assembled crowd was thrilled as they watched Miss Sadie Creswell, assistant cashier of the Flathead County State Bank of Polson, board the plane and accompany Mr Maroney as a passenger on his second flight.

Maroney, who had earlier set a state endurance record by remaining in the air for 43 minutes, returned to the Flathead on August 10th and put on another air show. He left for Butte shortly thereafter, and never returned to the reservation Many years passed before any other airmen came into the area

A flight in an airplane was a great thrill, and early-day pilots often "set up shop" at celebrations and gatherings, offering plane rides to the braver souls Walter H Brown, a pilot from Missoula, brought his plane to Polson and offered flights in conjunction with a rodeo which was held on August 6th and 7th in 1927 On the first day, many passengers were delighted with their sky rides which originated from a field across the river from town

On the second day, Brown changed fields, and took off from a field just east of the dump ground Frank

First seaplane flight in northwest recorded at Polson, 1913

Phil Timm, manager-operator Polson and Lake county
airports, 1962

(Flathead Courier Photo)

Mast, a mechanic, and his fiance, Cora Simonsen, were the passengers on the first flight of the afternoon Taking off in northerly direction, the plane just cleared the telephone wires, but hit a tall radio aerial pole, breaking the pole in half. The damaged plane crashed headlong over the river bank and came to a jarring stop against a large rock at the water's edge. Walter H. Brown, the pilot, escaped with only minor injuries, but the two passengers succumbed with a few hours.

Leslie Tower left his name in the annals of aviation In 1910, his father, Ralph R. Tower, was homestead entrant number 9, and eight-year-old Leslie began his life on the reservation He graduated from Polson High School with the class of 1922, and then took an engineering course at the University of Washington. In 1927, Leslie Tower took up aviation in the army, making flights from three different army air fields Following his army duty, he joined the staff of the Boeing Company in Seattle as a draftsman-engineer. Making rapid advancement, he soon became Boeing's chief test pilot

Sent abroad to sell and demonstrate the company's aircraft, Tower astounded French onlookers as he flew the plane upside-down over vineyards In 1935, he was called home from a trip to Spain to take controls of the first B-17, the Flying Fortress, that the Boeing Company had built at a cost of half a million dollars

His ability as a test pilot was invaluable He was capable of flying planes of any size, could test them in the air, and not only ascertain if there was a defect in the operation of the plane, but could advise the engineers on how to remedy the defect.

In the early part of October, 1935, after thoroughly testing the B-17, Leslie flew the big bomber from Seattle to an army airfield at Dayton, Ohio His flying time, averaging 300 miles an hour, was 6 hours, 45 minutes and was considered a record The Boeing pilot put the B-17 through all the tests required by the army engineers at the air base, and they were satisfied with the plane's maneuvers

On October 31, 1935, army engineers asked Tower to accompany the army pilots on a trial flight of the Flying Fortress When the plane reached an altitude of 100 feet, it quivered and Tower rushed to remedy the trouble, but he was too late The plane crashed, and fire immediately broke out Leslie Tower was pulled from the wreckage, badly burned, and passed away three weeks later, on November 21, 1935 Investigation listed the cause of the crash as "locked controls."

Tower's body was flown home by the Boeing Company, accompanied by his brother, Harold Tower, and the Boeing chief engineer The Tower funeral was the largest ever held in Polson, with a Methodist minister and a Catholic priest officiating The airman was laid to rest on the hill overlooking the Flathead Lake In eight years of flying, Leslie Tower did not have a minor accident to mar his record At the time of his death, top Boeing officials stated that he had no equal among airmen of the United States

With the steady advancement of aeronautics, the city of Polson soon became air-minded In April, 1928, an aviation field for Polson was approved by the city voters with a margin of seven votes Steps were taken to purchase forty acres of land across the river, one-half mile west of town On February 28, 1931, the final payment on the land was made, and a deed was executed by J F McAlear and Olive G McAlear to the city of Polson for what is now the Polson Air Field

148

In addition to the forty acres bought, the city secured a long-term lease on the adjoining tract, and a passable runway was built This municipal airport was the first field on the reservation The first reservation pilot to own his own plane was Hoyt Demers of Arlee, son of Louis Demers, a reservation pioneer Hoyt Demers made good use of his plane and of the Polson airport when he flew in to play on the Polson baseball team.

On February 5, 1943, the Polson Airport gained some notoriety and was the scene of feverish activity During the evening, residents of the town heard a large plane circling the city as if trying to get its bearings Sensing that the plane was lost, some of the local people drove their cars to the airfield and lined the edges of the airstrip, turning the car lights toward the center to illuminate the runway. The B-17, originally based at Walla Walla, Washington, glided in from the north, landed on the lighted runway, and came to a stop in big drifts of snow at the end of the field. Just beyond the drifts of snow was a ravine which could have dropped the Flying Fortress into the river. The plane had enough gas for another five minutes of flying time

The crew, thinking they were in Idaho, were quite surprised to learn they were in Polson, Montana They removed the top-secret Norden bombsight from the plane, and it was sealed in the vault at the Security State Bank. The people of Polson opened their hearts and homes to the crew while they were stationed in the town, awaiting a veteran bomber pilot from Walla Walla and improved conditions at the airfield which would enable them to take off The runway was cleared as much as possible, and lengthened somewhat with the removal of two fences.

When the field was ready, talk flew through the town that the plane would take off the following morning at 9 30. Superintendent I. E. White of the high school called a special assembly for all students and admonished them, telling them that absolutely no one would be excused in order to see the Flying Fortress take off.

The next morning, there was a mass exodus of townspeople and students to the airfield. Included in the crowd, with a sheepish grin on his face, was a man who had just autographed the B-17, I E. White, Superintendent of Schools, Polson, Montana

The big ship roared down the runway, and took off with fifty feet to spare where the fences had been, returning to the wild blue yonder The townspeople returned to their jobs and homes, and the students and Mr. White returned to the high school

Since 1943, aeronautical development on the reservation has moved forward. There are four airfields on the reservation at the present time In Sanders county, the Hot Springs Airport is controlled by the County of Sanders and is managed by the Town of Hot Springs The three airfields in Lake county — St. Ignatius, Ronan and Polson — are supervised by the Lake County Joint Airport Board Members of this board include Millo Jensen and Don Olsson of Ronan; Chester Hilton of St Ignatius; and Elmore Viehman and Eddie Pinkney, Jr., of Polson.

The operator and manager of the Lake county fields is Phil Timm of Polson, who has an inspector's rating. The Timm Aero Service at Polson features rental, maintenance, air taxi service, and student training. There are three planes available for use, one of which is the only sea plane in the state of Montana The Polson airfield

150

has year-round services, and in the summer months can handle D-C 3's and Queen Aire planes

The interest in flying is becoming more widespread. Owners of planes on the reservation include Grant Preston of Hot Springs, the Glory B and the Boher Ranch, with Roy Knutson, manager, and The Mission Flyers, all of St. Ignatius; Lyle Dupuis of Ronan; Alvie Leighton, W. E. Pinkney, Jr, Oliver Dupuis, Will Tiddy, Jr, The Flathead Lake Flyers Club, Fred Varnum, Darrell Even, A. H. Rowley, Bob Atkinson, C S Webb, and the Timm Aero Service, all of Polson

When Phil Timm first came to the reservation in 1956, there were 480 flying activities logged at the Lake county fields In 1961, there were 3,320 flying activities recorded.

The birds in the skways of the Flathead no longer have a monopoly on the view from overhead as man takes to the air, likes it, and looks for newer horizons.

The "Twist" — Montana-style, 1962 Diamond J-C Rodeo, Polson

(Flathead Courier Photo)

CHAPTER SIXTEEN
Lake County

When the reservation was opened for white settlement in 1910, it lay in parts of Sanders, Missoula, and Flathead counties. Approximately one-fourth of it was in Sanders county and the remainder, the eastern portion, was in Missoula and Flathead counties

As the reservation grew in population and wealth, there was an agitation for the formation of a new county. The center of the reservation, just north of the townsite of Pablo, was a great distance from either county seat — Missoula and Kalispell — and it was felt that the reservation area was not properly served county-wise.

In 1922, the agitation began to take the form of forceful action as both Ronan and Polson vied for the honor of becoming the county seat of the area to be formed into a possible new county. The only agreement reached was that the new county would be named Lake if it were formed

One man who actively took part in the creation of the new county in general, and the naming of Polson as county seat in particular, was lumber man Ben Cramer. Ben stomped throughout the reservation country, tolling the virtues and pleading the cause Others from Polson who were active in the political battle were Father Wm. O'Malley, W J Burke, A J Lowary, F. H. Nash, and Z. B Silver Equally active, but carrying the banner for Ronan, were Tom Fisher, A. J. Brower, John P Swee, A. M Sterling, Stanley Scearce, and J. A. Lemire

In January, 1923, the commissioners of Flathead and Missoula counties agreed to an election which would let the voters living in the proposed new county decide on the proposition, and in the same election name the county seat as well as the first county officers. The election day was set for April 30, 1923

The following months found the reservation embroiled in arguments, discussions, and mass gatherings as the voters were wooed and persuaded by Polson and Ronan backers. April 30th finally arrived, and voters on the reservation flocked to the polls.

There wasn't much flocking at the Big Draw polling place, west of Elmo There were two judges and two clerks — Mr. and Mrs Paul Bower and Mr. and Mrs. Bud Bruns — and only five votes were cast in this precinct. One man in the vicinity rode five miles to vote, and then wasn't allowed to do so because he wasn't registered. When the election was over, the entire tally of the Big Draw precinct was disqualified and not allowed. The residence of Mr. and Mrs. Bruns, which was the polling place, was not on the reservation, they had illegally served on the election board, and had illegally voted since it was necessary that they be residents of the area affected by the election.

When the last vote had been tallied, and all the precincts had reported in, a new county had been formed with Polson as the county seat The official notice ran as follows:

"Affecting that part of the reservation in Flathead and Missoula, along with other areas in the Swan Valley and the area north of the reservation lines:

154

Precinct	Lake County		For County Seat	
	For	Against	Ronan	Polson
Arlee	59	139	85	109
Ravalli	15	34	24	24
St. Ignatius	203	249	274	171
Ronan No. 38	245	18	254	15
Ronan No. 42	87	5	92	0
Ronan No. 43	68	6	76	3
Ronan No. 44	117	5	119	4
Moiese	41	47	52	39
Horte-Round Butte	155	7	133	44
D'Aste	45	33	54	26
Pablo	195	19	101	115
Charlo	111	48	122	46
Woods Bay	16	14	10	20
Swan Lake	0	23	0	0
Swan River	0	31	2	2
Big Draw	2	3	0	5
Irvine Flats	68	20	4	87
Rollins	35	27	3	62
Garcon Gulch	24	14	15	25
Big Arm	44	15	1	56
Dayton	73	58	22	106
Polson No. 31	407	5	1	411
Grandview	367	10	19	363
Polson No. 38	244	2	2	245
Sunny Slope	74	1	0	74
Totals	2780	834	1466	2140

The first officers elected to serve in Lake County
were:
State Senator .... J. H. Lyle, Arlee
State Representative .... Frank L White, Seines
(Irvine Flats)
Commissioner — 6 yr. term George T. Farrell, chairman,
Pablo
Commissoner — 4 yr. term   Arthur T. Schmidt, Charlo
Commissioner — 2 yr. term   C. W. Weythman, Polson
Clerk & Recorder   M M Marcy, St. Ignatius
Clerk of the Court D. A. Cubbage ~~John McGrann, Big Arm~~
Assessor   Lyman C. Hall, Pablo
Sheriff   Wilbert R Kelly, St Ignatius
Treasurer   Carl Iverson, Pablo
County Attorney   Mark H Derr, Ronan
Supt of Schools   Mary E Eckstein, Ronan
Coroner   Christian J. Hoeschen, St. Ignatius

Lake County was thus created, and began to function
ninety days after the Flathead County Commissioners
canvassed the votes and certified the results of the election. The date, August 10, 1923, was a national holiday
due to the death of President Warren G Harding, so Lake
County began its official existence as a county of the
state of Montana on August 11, 1923

Lake County was without a court house and the
county offices were located in various buildings throughout Polson until 1934 At that time, after pressure from
political and business groups, the city of Polson gave a
warranty deed to the county commissioners, deeding
Block 18 to Lake County for the sum of $10, stipulating
that the ground was to be used by the county for court
house purposes. The deed, signed by B Joe Wilson, mayor,

and R B Davidson, clerk of the city of Polson, was dated December 4, 1934

Lake County began construction on the present courthouse soon thereafter, and the county officers moved into their new quarters on December 5, 1935.

And so it was that government of, for, and by the people came to the reservation

Buffalo riding in Missoula Stampede, 1915. Rider is Jim
Grinder. Ropers are Carl Davis, left, and Charley Allard

(Photo loaned by Tommy Pablo)

CHAPTER SEVENTEEN
The Playground of the Northwest

The Flathead Indian Reservation has always held a magnetic charm. The native Indians, who first inhabited the region, were appreciative and proud of the area which was a wild game paradise with an additional abundance of wild berries, fish, good grass, deep forests, and pure water.

Their pride was first demonstrated to the white man when they described the scenic beauty of the area to the fur-trader and explorer, David Thompson, in 1812. When Thompson's party was guided to the promised land, with the majestic Mission Mountain and the fabulous Flathead Lake, David Thompson marvelled, made surveys and notations, and later gave rapturous reports.

This was the beginning of an influx of travelers to the Flathead country. They included adventurers, fur-traders, missionaries, land agents, and settlers. The early immigration reached its peak when 81,363 people registered for homestead land on the reservation during the months of July and August in 1909.

The first man to see the immensity, and the commercial potential of the Flathead area as an attraction to tourists, was Colonel A A White of St. Paul, Minnesota. In 1915, the government held Villa Site sales, selling lots on the reservation for $10 to $25 an acre A choice two-acre site, at that time, brought an all-time high of $700 All of the 890 lots offered were sold, bringing the total receipts to more than $130,000

Colonel White purchased more than 400 Villa Sites, which included most of Wild Horse Island. The Colonel was a land speculator, and he paid one-fourth down, $18-000, on his lots then conducted an extensive sale campaign to interest buyers in his lake property. Prospective buyers were given free rides from Glacier National Park to the lake, and many other sales promotions were tried — to no avail. Few sales were made.

By 1923, Colonel White was badly in arrears with his payments to the government for the property, and reservation residents petitioned the U S Land Office to repossess the lots so they could be sold to others. The government finally settled with White, deeding to him 192 lots for the $18,000 he had originally paid down in 1915 Later, many of these lots were sold for taxes. Colonel White's vision of a summer wonderland for tourists was bright, but it was also thirty years too soon The government held another sale of the available sites in 1924, but only 23 lots were. sold. People said the prices — $50 to $100 an acre — were too high, and they wouldn't buy.

Since that time, however, the real estate development around the Flathead Lake has been spectacular. Many beautiful summer homes have been built, and lots that once sold for $50 now sell for $5,000 and more. Assisting in the development of the lake shore properties is Frank Hodge, son of Eugene Hodge, Sr , early-day boat captain. Frank keeps a crew busy eight months out of the year on the SS Hodge, a flat-bottom boat, with the building of docks, rip-rapping the shore line, and driving piling Walter Davis has a smaller flat-bottom boat, and he conducts the same type of business Both men have living quarters on their boats

In addition to the Flathead Lake, there are many points of interest for the tourist on the reservation, whether he wants to spend an entire summer or just thoroughly enjoy his two-week vacation. Among the attractions are the Bison Range, the St. Ignatius Mission

Church, Hot Springs mineral baths, the Mission Mountain range with its many streams, Kerr Dam, the Mission and McDonald Lakes, Blue Bay Resort, Yellow Bay, the University of Montana Biological Station, and the recreation park at Polson.

Going hand-in-hand with tourism is swimming, boating, skiing, and golfing The highlight of the swimming season on the reservation is the Red Cross swimming instruction program which is conducted at the recreation beach near Polson during July of each year. Over 600 children participate in this program which teaches swimming skills and water safety The children are transported from St. Ignatius, Ronan, Charlo, Moiese, Polson, and outlying areas by school bus. Upon completion of the course, certificates are awarded to the swimmers

You seldom see a body of water without a boat, and the Flathead Lake is no exception. Boating is a very popular recreation during the summer, both for tourists and local residents Many boats ply the waters of the Flathead, from small rowboats to runabouts and cabin cruisers. In recent years, the water sport of skiing has become more popular, and the Flathead Lake accommodates this sport quite well.

The climax of the boating season is the annual Copper Cup Regatta at Polson, which is held on the third weekend of August. The event is sponsored by the Polson Jaycees, and it attracts competitors from all over the northwest. It is open to outboard racing boats and limited inboards — those which have a piston displacement of 266 to 280 cubic inches. This boating classic was first held in 1934, and has become more popular each year.

Three individuals who have made names for themselves with their racing boats are W E. Pinkney, Jr.,

Ray Boettcher, and Oliver Dupuis. In 1954, Oliver Dupuis held the national championship in the Service C Hydro class of racing boats.

Golfing is another popular summer recreation, and the nine-hole course just east of Polson is considered one of the best in the state Clubs are available for rental to visitors, and the greens are kept in top condition. The course and recreation park which adjoins is municipally owned by the City of Polson Lin Storti is the golf pro and manager in charge of the course

Keeping pace with the tourist demand, there is a total of 150 units in motels and tourist courts, and there are accommodations for house trailers Many of the courts have boating and skiing facilities for their patrons

Ten reservoirs and numerous streams on the reservation abound in game fish that delight the heart of a fisherman. One of the most popular fishing spots is the Nine Pipe Reservoir which is well-known for its black bass. Allentown, which is popular for fishing and the fall hunting of ducks, geese, and pheasant, was founded by Mrs Marge Allen in 1953 It is now owned and operated by G F Perry and Louie Luhman, and offers motel accommodations for the outdoorsman.

There is an open season for fishing the year-round on the Flathead Lake The lake has the distinction of yielding the largest fish ever caught in Montana waters. On May 28, 1955, a white sturgeon, 7½ feet long and weighing 181 pounds, was caught near Wild Horse Island. The white sturgeon are bottom-feeders and get their food at night Although none have been caught and landed since, many people have seen the big sturgeon in the lake. In September of 1955, a group of thirty people saw a school of the sturgeon near White's Lookout Point, north of Rollins

162

The waters of the reservation provide the fisherman with such bounty as mackinaw, rainbow, Dolly Varden, salmon, whitefish, bass, and perch. If the fisherman isn't alert, and misses his catch, he can always return with a tale of the big one that got away.

— **Sports** —

During the early settlement of the reservation, baseball was the favorite sport Towns would vie with each other for the best ball-playing talent available. The competition was keen, and quite often players were imported for crucial games.

Rodeos were also very popular, and every Sunday during the summer, a rodeo — large or small — was held somewhere on the reservation. The Indians were skilled horsemen, and more often than not, they rode off with the prize money. In addition to the events in bronco riding, bulldogging, bull-riding, and calf roping, the rodeo was made more exciting with the dangerous pastime of riding buffalo.

One of the most colorful cowboys to hit the sod in a rodeo arena was a half-breed Nez Perce Indian, Jim Grinder His most spectacular ride was performed in 1915, when he rode the toughest and wildest buffalo available at the Missoula Stampede Although fracturing two ribs on the first day of the rodeo, when a bad buffalo threw him, Jim returned the next day and rode a wild shaggy bull to a standstill Jim Grinder is now past 91 years old, and makes his home in Missoula

Football and basketball have been popular sports during the past fifty years, with accent on high school competition The first high school football game ever played on the reservation was held on a Saturday afternoon on October 23, 1915, in Polson A field was marked off and upright posts were set up at either end The Flathead County High School Braves met the Polson High School team, and the Braves met defeat with a score of 27-7 This was the only time that a Flathead team was beaten by Polson The Polson squad consisted of twelve players, but the reserve man was kept on the bench and didn't see action in the game In the early-day rough and tumble sport, the coach feared he might get injured In 1948, a six-man football team fielded by St. Ignatius won the Class C state championship They had twenty-three players on the squad

Basketball is perhaps the most popular high school sport, and it is played much faster today than it was when the reservation schools first started competing In 1956, St Ignatius won the Class B state championship in basketball, and in 1960, Ronan took the first place honors. The class B teams on the reservation are St Ignatius, Ronan, and Polson, the class C teams include Charlo, Hot Springs, Dixon, and Arlee

Competition in track has always been keen on the reservation, and while many individual performances have been recorded, only one team has ever won first place honors at the Interscholastic Meet held in Missoula in May of each year Polson High School won the championship in 1952, 1955, and 1956. The fastest time ever recorded at the state meet in the 880 yard run — 1:52 2 — was put in the books by a Polson athlete, Mike Stark, in May, 1961 Mike graduated from Polson High with the Class of 1962

Another sport which is attracting more and more enthusiasts is bowling Reservation bowlers has two establishments at their disposal — one in Ronan and one in Polson In addition to league competition, both lanes

Ronan Chiefs, State "B" Basketball Champions, 1960 From left, Homer Courville, Ronald Richwine, Adrian Gohl, Frank Arlint, James Hurt, Duane Martin, Harold Fullerton, John Lindberg, Ken Dresen, Leonard Shocker, Gary Bocksnick, Roger Cheff. Kneeling is Coach Arthur Previs.

1956 State Class B Champions, St. Ignatius. Standing from left to right are Coach Keith Clawson, Fred Blackman, Bill Hilton, Jim Saylor, Louis Blood, Bill Whalen, Jim Pinsonault, Asst. Coach Joe Eslick. Sitting, from left, are Garry Marcum, Ken Phillips, Miki Corcoran, Bap Incashoula, and Lou Incashoula

sponsor invitational tournaments for men and women which attract bowlers throughout the northwest.

The most outstanding athlete on the reservation during the past fifty years is Archie McDonald, son of Tom and Christine McDonald, and grandson of the early-day fur-trader, Angus McDonald. Born near St. Ignatius on January 22, 1896, Archie was a typical reservation mixture, having Scotch, Nez Perce, Blackfoot, and Spanish blood running through his veins. Standing six feet tall and weighing 180 pounds, Archie was a natural, colorful athlete. He attended the Chemawa Indian School in Tekoa, Washington, and excelled in football, basketball, and such track events as sprinting, high jump, broad jump, pole vault, shot-put, and discus and javelin throw.

In reservation baseball, he was outstanding and versatile, having played every position on the team at one time or another during his ball career. Like his father, Archie McDonald was an expert horseman, winning first-place money quite often as a bronc-buster. He hit the peak of his rodeo career at the Mission Stampede when he rode "Coyote," a bad bronc that had never been ridden before.

Archie McDonald is now retired, and is making his home in St. Ignatius with his wife, Sophie Dumont McDonald.

Polson high school track star, Mike Stark, left, and Coach Tom Kingsford

CHAPTER EIGHTEEN
Schools — Hospitals — Churches
— Schools —

During the early settlement of the reservation, schools were few and far between, and school houses were even less in existence. Classes were held in whatever buildings were available, and there wasn't a high school in existence on the entire reservation. By 1911, with most of the land occupied by homesteaders, there were many country schools scattered throughout the area. The first high school was built in Polson, the largest town on the reservation, and this school accommodated freshmen, sophomores, and seniors.

As time progressed, and population increased, there were high schools at Hot Springs, Lone Pine, Dixon, Arlee, St. Ignatius, Leon, Charlo, Ronan, Round Butte, and Pablo. Today, due to modern transportation facilities available to rural students, the high schools of Lone Pine, Leon, Round Butte, and Pablo are no longer in

First motor-powered school bus on reservation, Polson

(Meiers Studio Photo)

existence Their high school students are transported to the schools in the nearby larger towns

Country schools, which once were so numerous, now number only eight Camas Prairie, Niarada, Dayton, Elmo, Valley View, Moiese, Round Butte, and Pablo At one time there were forty-four districts on the reservation which offered the basic courses of education Today, with a streamlined fifteen school districts, the students have a more rounded curriculum to choose from, including vocational and commercial courses

The following facts and figures are in regard to the reservation schools

— Country Schools — 1962 —

School	Pupils	Faculty	Principal
Camas Prairie	46	Irene Ulvick	
		Gertrude Bulger	
Dayton	17	Rita Grant	
Elmo	27	Mildred Grant	
		Warren Hirst	
Valley View	33	Ruth Irish	
		Mary Rowton	
Round Butte	80	four teachers	Floyd Bond
Moiese	40	two teachers	Ben Jakes
Pablo	138	five teachers	Richard McCrea
Niarada	7	Willa Huckins	

— High School Districts, 1962 —

Arlee — Larry Ryan is the Superintendent of Schools of the district There are 216 pupils in the elementary school and 84 high school students. The district owns four 60-passenger school busses The faculty members number fifteen for both schools in the district

Dixon — Superintendent of Schools in the Dixon district is Thomas S Duffy The faculty is composed of

168

six elementary teachers and five high school teachers. In the elementary school there are 105 pupils, and the high school enrollment reaches 34 The district has four school busses

Hot Springs — District No 14 has 187 elementary students and 96 high school students Earl Barlow is the Superintendent of Schools, and Roy Snyder began work at the school as the custodian in 1933, and is still on the payroll. The faculty numbers fifteen, with eight elementary teachers and seven high school teachers. Of the seven school busses which transport the students, two of them are district owned.

Charlo — There are 200 students at the elementary level, and 105 students at the high school level who are taught by eight elementary teachers and seven high school teachers E. B McCurdy is the Superintendent of Schools.

St. Ignatius — The pupils in the elementary system number 375, and the high school attendance reaches 162. Fifteen teachers teach the lower grades, and there are eight high school teachers Stuart Fitschen is the Superintendent of Schools.

Ronan — Twelve teachers are in charge of the education of 245 students in the high school, and seventeen teachers handle the teaching assignments at the elementary level, with 515 students in attendance A. L. Cooper is the Superintendent of Schools.

The schools of Ronan, St. Ignatius, Charlo Pablo, Moiese, and Round Butte compose school district No. 28. This district has 24 school busses which handle the transportation for all of the schools

Polson — David R Pugh has been an instructor and principal of the high school since 1937, and is still continuing in that capacity. Francis Bartlett has held the same dual position in the elementary school, also since 1937. There are 717 pupils in the elementary school, with 27 teachers; and 343 pupils in the high school, with 18 teachers. S. Clay Coy is the Superintendent of Schools, and George Sager has been the school custodian since 1935. There are 12 school busses used for transportation of students from the rural areas.

At the county level of the education system, Muriel Hamman is the County Superintendent of the Lake County schools, and Orrin Kendall of Thompson Falls is the Sanders County Superintendent of Schools.

The oldest established school on the reservation is the Villa Ursula, the parochial school at St. Ignatius under the supervision of the Ursuline Sisters, with Mother Magdalene La Tranch in charge. The present brick structure of the school was constructed in 1922, and consisted of eight classrooms and five dining rooms. Of the 150 students who attend the grade school classes, 75 of them are non-residential who board and room at the school. Many of the food products used by the school cooks are produced on the farm which belongs to the Jesuit Fathers at the Mission.

— Hospitals —

The first hospital on the reservation was established in 1864 at St. Ignatius by four nuns, Sisters of the Providence, who came to Montana from Oregon. The hospital has been in continuous operation since that year. In 1962, a modern, up-to-date building was constructed at a cost of $800,000 to house The Holy Family Hospital which accommodates thirty patients. Sister Joseph Arthur is the administrator of the Religious Hospitallers; Dr. F. L. Van Veen is the resident physician and surgeon, and Dr. J. Murray Brooke of Ronan also cares for patients at the medical sanctuary.

The Sanders County General Hospital at Hot Springs was constructed in 1950 at a cost of $256,000. The money for the county hospital was obtained through popular subscription, two bond issues, and a grant under the Hill-Burton Act of Congress. It is a nineteen-bed, two story hospital, and is considered to be one of the finest small hospitals in the state of Montana. Operated by Sanders County, the hospital is under the administration of Mr. Denegar.

The St. Luke Community Hospital in Ronan is a one-story, 23-bed structure which was begun in March, 1953. Hard work and perseverance by community leaders, and the support of the townspeople in popular subscription and benefit affairs has enabled the Center City and its surrounding area to reap the benefits and advantages of a community hospital.

The directors of the hospital are: Cal Nielson, chairman; Dr. R. D. Read, Stanley Scearce, Jr., William Phillips, John Cornelius, Mrs. Bob Gilchrist, and Mrs. Clyde Clary, secretary. Mrs. Frank Mager is the managing supervisor. Consulting physicians and surgeons include: Dr. J. M. Brooke, Dr. S. T. McDonald of Ronan, Dr. W. G. Tanglin of Polson, and Dr. William J. Little, radiologist of Kalispell who consults one day a week.

On February 1, 1915, Miss Byrnes — a registered nurse — and Mrs. Landerback — a practical nurse — established the first hospital in Polson in a two-story home. The Polson General Hospital had a surgical room, a nursery, and rooms for six patients. The attending doctors of this pioneer hospital were George B. Owen and Dr. William J. Marshall.

Up to this time, people couldn't get sick as there was no hospital to accommodate them. With the opening of

171

the Polson General Hospital, six people could get sick at one time.

Rev Father William O'Maley, resident pastor of the Immaculate Conception Church of Polson, seeing the urgent need for a better hospital, went to Canada seeking help. He induced Mother St Joseph, Sister Mary of the Sacred Heart, and Sister Gertrude Leahy, Religious Hospitallers, to come to Polson.

They arrived in Polson on August 28, 1916, took over the Polson General Hospital, and quickly had the building remodeled. Re-named The Hotel Dieu Hospital, it opened on September 20, 1916, and the first patient admitted and cared for was an Indian.

In 1922, the A. M. Davidson home was purchased by the Sisters, and in 1933 a thirty-bed, three story brick building was constructed on the site. In 1957, a new hospital plant was constructed adjacent to the original hospital which accommodated forty patients The older building remained in use, and seventy people could get sick in the Polson area and receive competent hospital care. The value of the present plant, now called St. Joseph Hospital, is over one million dollars.

Sister St. Joseph is the Administrator The consulting physicians and surgeons are Dr. H. M. Teel, Dr. W. G. Tanglin, Dr. Ward Benkelman, and Dr. Earl D. Coriell. Dr. W. J. Little, radiologist of Kalispell, makes weekly visits.

As of January 1, 1962, the sum of $143,349.25 had been raised by popular subscription with community efforts. The Hospital Advisory Board officers who were largely responsible for the benefit drives and other work involved were E. E. Funke, Advisory Board Chairman; Ernest Klepetko, Planning & Development Chairman;

St. Joseph Hospital at Polson

Ralph R. Tower, Campaign Chairman; Norin T. Johnson, Campaign Treasurer; and Sister St. Joan of Arc, administrator of the New Addition Hospital.

— Churches —

The first church was established on the reservation in 1854, when the Black Robes founded the St. Ignatius Mission. Since that time, the Catholic Fathers have administered spiritually to the Indians on the reservation and to all other races continuously to the present time. The second church on the reservation was established at the Jocko Agency. In 1909, Catholic churches were located at Polson, with Rev. Father Griva, and at Ronan, in 1910, with Rev. Father O'Malley. A few years later, Catholic churches were erected at Hot Springs, Dixon, and D'Aste.

With the vanguard of white settlers arriving in 1909, many of whom were of the Protestant faith, there was a need for Protestant services. Rev. O. A. White of Kalispell, District Superintendent of the Methodist Church, conducted the first Protestant services in the Mansur Hardware store building in Polson in September, 1909.

173

1910, the Methodist Church built the first Protestant church in Polson, and it is still in use at the present time. Soon thereafter, this religious organization built and established churches in Ronan, St. Ignatius, Arlee, Dixon, Charlo, and Round Butte. The pastors who are presently serving in these reservation communities are Loy Estes, Polson; Arthur Heath, Ronan, Charlo, and Round Butte, and John Nolan, St. Ignatius, Arlee, and Dixon.

Other Protestant churches on the reservation, and their pastors:

Presbyterian — Polson, Dr. W. D. Copeland; Hot Springs, Rev. Donald Simmonds.

Community Presbyterian — Lone Pine, Rev. Donald Simmonds; Dayton, Rev. Donald Simmonds.

Lutheran, American — Ronan, Rev. John Olson; Polson, Rev. Donald Jacobson.

Trinity Lutheran — Hot Springs, Rev. Lars O. Lasseson.

Lutheran, Mo. Synod — Pablo, Rev. E. W. Krause; St. Ignatius, Rev. E. W. Krause.

Church of Jesus Christ of Latter Day Saints — Polson, Joseph Priest, Bishop; Charlo, Everett Foust, Bishop; St. Ignatius, Ray Jensen, Bishop.

The Christian Church — Polson, Rev. James Morgan.

The Christian Church (Independent) — Ronan, Rev. Dewey Obenchaine; St. Ignatius, Rev. Robert Larsson.

Assembly of God Church — Ronan, Rev. Leon Mitchell; Polson, Rev. John Weaver.

Christian & Missionary Alliance — Ronan, Rev. M. R. Erdman; Arlee, Rev. Robert Mallory; St. Ignatius, Rev. Robert Mallory.

First Baptist Church — Polson, Rev. Zane E. Bull.

Grace Baptist Church — Polson, Rev. Ronald Stabbert.

Church of the Reformation — Polson, Rev. Donald K. Dale.

Reorganized Church of Jesus Christ of Latter Day Saints — Polson, Rev. Murl Axtell.

St. Andrew's Episcopal — Polson, Rev. Father Richard Turner.

Nazarene Church — Pablo, Rev. Albert Miller; Hot Springs, Rev. Ava Bainter.

Bible Church — Moiese, Keith Rankin, pastor.

Christian Science Society — Polson, Eva Walker, First Reader.

Catholic — Ronan, D'Aste, Rev. Father Bernard McCarthy; St. Ignatius, Rev. Father Michael Shannon; Arlee, Rev. Father Geis; Dixon, Rev. Father Byrne; Polson, Rev. Father Leonard Jensen.

Holy Family Hospital — Polson, Rev. Father John J. O'Kennedy.

Church of Christ — Polson, no pastor as present.

Seventh Day Adventist — Polson, No pastor at present.

Interior view of Mission church murals
(Meiers Studio Photo)

175

Partial view of Polson business section, 1910

(Wasson Photo)

First carload shipment of 1914 model Fords at Polson

CHAPTER NINETEEN
Towns of the Reservation
— Polson —

Long before the white man created the reservation, the area where the town of Polson now stands was known by the Salish Indians as Pied e'lai or "foot of the lake."

In 1880, Harry Lambert settled at "the foot of the lake" and began operating a general merchandise store. The store building was a log cabin structure, and was located across the street and south of the present Salish Hotel site. At this time the community became known as Lambert's Landing. Batiste Eneas, a great-grandfather of Emma Davis Dupuis of the Flathead Agency, put into service a ferry boat which was constructed of long cedar poles. This ferry plied the river just north of the present Polson bridge

In and about 1888, Harry Lambert sold his store to Joe Theoa who in turn sold out to Henry Therriault in 1893 Henry built a bigger and better headquarters for his store, and constructed a hotel where the Salish Hotel is now located.

Between 1890 and 1897, the towns on the reservation enjoyed the growth and development of a new country There were post offices established in Arlee, St Ignatius, Ravalli, Dayton, and Ronan, but Lambert's Landing had no post office One had been approved for the settlement, but no name had been selected The settlers in the area appointed Batiste Eneas and David Polson to give the new post office a name The two men got together and after much discussion, David Polson suggested they use the name of Eneas Batiste Eneas hastily declined the honor, and recommended they call it Polson, believing it to be a better name for a town

David Polson was born in New Haven, Conneticut, in 1826 of Scottish parentage. In 1849, he joined the Gold Rush and migrated to California, working his way with a string of pack horses. He later found himself in Carson City, Nevada. In 1861, he went by pack train to Walla Walla, Washington, and thence on to Orofino, Idaho. In Idaho he married a Nez Perce Indian, Mary Kane, and to this union was born a daughter, Agnes. In 1863, David Polson and his family crossed the Lolo Pass into the Bitter Root Valley with a hunting party of the Nez Perce. Polson settled in the Bitter Root until 1870, when he moved to the reservation and located on a ranch five miles northwest of Lambert's Landing. David Polson engaged in stock raising, and became very popular with the Flathead Indians. He was much in demand as a fiddler at the dances and pow wows. David Polson died in 1902, just four years after the town of Polson had been named for him.

The Polson Post Office was established on January 22, 1898, and Henry Therriault, owner of the general store and hotel, was the first postmaster. The present-day postmaster is J. Roy Cramer.

In 1900, Therriault sold his business to Fred Corbin. Two years later it was purchased by Charles Allard, Jr. and Oscar Sedman. In 1904, F L. Gray and F. P. Browne of Kalispell bought the business buildings of Polson and F. L. Gray was named the postmaster. The following year, J. L. McIntire of Kalispell joined the firm which was called The F. L. Gray Company. The business buildings were enlarged and included the store, the postoffice, and the Grandview Hotel In 1909, with the opening of the reservation at hand, the company started construction on a large building which was located where the

Federated Store, Davis Merc., and Lloyd's Variety Store now stand. The F. L. Gray Company moved into their new building on July 4, 1910, and this called for an added celebration for the growing town.

Polson grew by leaps and bounds in 1910, with the influx of settlers forcing the growth. By September 1, almost one thousand residents populated the young settlement.

The following are memorable dates for the city of Polson:

April 5, 1910 — The town of Polson was incorporated, with 300 people voting in the election.

May 23, 1910 — The first election of city officers was held and the following were put into office: C. M. Mansur, mayor; W. W. Gabb, J. C. Chambers, J. J. McDonald, C. L. Wright, J. M. Dawson, and H. A. Kaiser were the councilmen.

June 10, 1910 — The first meeting of the city officials was held and the city government was organized.

June 15, 1912 —James Harbert of Kalispell bought the building and stock of the Kaiser-McCann store. He was an ardent booster for the Flathead, Polson, and irrigation. Shortly after locating in Polson, Jimmie Harbert unintentionally drove his new Buick car through the door of Eric Stahlberg's Public Garage. It didn't damage the car, but it required a full day of work to repair the garage door. Autos did have power drive, even in 1912.

October 15, 1912 — J. H. Cline and sons, Owen and Norman, purchased the first wheat and made the first sack of flour in the first major industry in Polson.

July, 1913 — The Polson Creamery, under the management of C. H. Matravers and A. L. Meek, produced the first butter.

May, 1914 — L. L. Marsh bought the Polson Creamery Company During peak production of the plant, 10 to 12,000 pounds of butter were produced under the direction of Otto Marsh, who was the buttermaker from 1915 until 1953 The Marshes employed ten to twelve men in the creamery. For many years, the Clines with their flour mill, and the Marshes with their creamery were the bread-and-butter men of the area.

April, 1914 — O'Connell and Wade opened the first Model T Ford agency A year later, Z B Silver, Polson's first auctioneer, sold his livery barn to C T Belknap, and took over the Ford Agency.

July, 1914 — The Dewey Lumber Company began the manufacture of lumber. It employed fifty men for more than thirty years, and was Polson's largest employer during that period.

Men who have served the city of Polson as mayor include: T. L. McMichael, J M. Dawson, J. W. Clark, W. H. B. Carter, L. L Marsh, Frank Stone, R. H. Gillam, W. J. Marshall, H S Hanson, James Harbert, B. Joe Wilson, J. H. Cline, M M Marcy, Oliver R Brown, E D. Pearce, S. W. Grinde, Mark H Derr, Sam P. Smith, Earl D. Coriell, and the present mayor, D. G. Ellenwood, Sr.

The city has its own water system which brings mountain water into town from the Mission Mountains on the east There is a city library Most of the streets in town are covered with black-top surfacing.

Polson has one of the best volunteer fire departments in the state with a rating comparable to that of a city much larger in size — 6th class.

Due to an alert fire department in 1912, a major disaster was avoided One January evening, Fred Jette was riding his horse down Main Street when he glanced

Polson, the city at the foot of the lake, 1962

(Meiers Studio Photo)

Swimming instruction at Polson beach

(Flathead Courier Photo)

through the window of the Dawson Furniture Store and saw flames. Fred galloped across the street to the Club Pool Hall, and voiced a loud alarm. Bill Keller and two other men responded and, with Jette, rushed to the fire department's hand-drawn hose cart which was in the alley to the east of the pool hall. The snow was deep, and the three men could hardly budge the cart. Gripping the hose cart with one hand, and the horse's tail with the other, they soon had the cart on the way to the nearest fire plug. Their quick action saved the adjoining buildings on either side of the furniture store. While the city has lost a building or two by fire, no disastrous fires have wiped out an entire city block or major area.

The vast development which has taken place in the Polson area during the past fifty years is reflected in the statements of the total assets of the banks of the city. On June 1, 1913, the combined total assets of the three banks in Polson — The Flathead County State Bank, $45,699.82; The First National Bank, $73,973.79; and the Security State Bank, $76,309.26 — amounted to $195,-982.87. On March 26, 1962, the total assets of the one bank which conducts business in Polson, the Security State Bank, were $4,937,570.87. J. H. Hanson, son of the co-founder of the bank, H. S. Hanson, is the bank president. Thelma Herman, daughter of co-founder J. A. Johnson, is assistant cashier in the bank.

Population-wise, in 1908, there were 300 people living within the city limits. According to the 1960 census, Polson had a population of 2,314, with 1,000 people living in the suburbs.

Polson Fire Department — well trained, well equipped.
(Flathead Courier Photo)

Bill Keller, 1962, shows cart he pulled in 1912 as fireman
(Meiers Studio Photo)

184

— Ronan —

The city of Ronan lies in the center of a rich agricultural area and for many years has been a trade center for the farmers of the lower Flathead and Mission valleys.

In 1883, with a small trading post as the nucleus of the settlement, it was known as Spring Creek — named for the creek that flowed through the town. In 1885, the government constructed a flour mill and a saw mill at the site, and the name was changed to Ronan Springs, in honor of the Indian agent, Peter Ronan, who served the Indians so well from 1873 to 1892.

The building of the Great Northern Railway increased the activity on the reservation, and on October 4, 1894, a post office was established to handle the increased demand for mail facilities. The name of the settlement was shortened to Ronan, and Ludger C. Tuott became the first postmaster. Knute Johnson is the present-day postmaster of the Ronan post office.

In 1905, A. M. Sterling took over the trading post, received a government Indian Trader's license, and established the A. M. Sterling Company. He enlarged the

Ronan, one-year-old, 1910

(Bigelow Photo)

185

Ronan, the "Center City," at it is in 1962

(Meiers Studio Photo)

store and built the Sterling Hotel, and became the first major business man of the area.

In 1908-09, many other businessmen became established in the Center City — Joseph and Ross Lemire, Frank Menager, J. F O'Brien, Pablo & Potvin, A. J. Brower, and others. Stanley Scearce came from the Klondike country in Alaska and built a general merchandise store which contained 6,000 square feet of floor space. By 1910, Ronan was booming, and soon had a population of over 500 residents.

But the town met disaster on August 24, 1912 A fire broke out in the automobile garage of Crawford & Clairmont during one of the fiercest wind storms of the season, and before the town could be alarmed, the fire had spread to other buildings. Willing men were ready to fight the inferno, but the chemical engine was not charged. By the time the engine was charged and ready for action, half the town was in flames and the other half was threatened.

Fire fighters carried water in buckets, tubs, and barrels from Spring Creek, but in vain. The fire spread across the street, destroying buildings in its path. The wind was so strong that it carried a piece of burning rubberoid roofing a quarter of a mile, and set the government flour mill on fire.

When the smoke had cleared, there were four buildings still standing west of Spring Creek — The Ronan Pioneer Building, Lemire Bros Store, the J. F. O'Brien General Store, and a millinery shop Destroyed were The Glacier Drug Store, Dr. Sheen's office, the Ronan State Bank, the Flathead Valley State Bank, and Stanley Scearce's large general store. The east side of the Creek was untouched except for the flour mill Smoky, but

safe, were the Sterling store and hotel, Menager's Dry
Goods, the Edmondson Pool Hall, Bateman's Livery
Barn, Burland's blacksmith shop and the Bigelow Photo-
graph Gallery.

Undaunted, the burned-out business men set about
to re-build the town. Stanley Scearce erected a 9,000
square-foot brick building on a site away from other
buildings. Others followed suit, such as The Reservation Land and Lumber Company which constructed its
building and yard at the edge of town. Stanley Scearce,
Inc. did a big volume of business, but in 1928, fire struck
again and burned the business to the ground. Still not
discouraged, Scearce re-built — this time on Central
Avenue — and the brick building still stands today, with
the business under the management of Stanley Scearce,
Jr.

The A. M Sterling Company continued to improve
their building structures and their business. After the
death of the senior Sterling, his son, Robert Sterling,
continued with the business which is now known as the
Sterling Shopping Center.

In 1916, Z. B. Silver and J L. Jones formed a partnership, built a fireproof brick garage, The Ronan Garage
Company, and opened the first Ford Auto agency in
Ronan. This firm is still in business, and is operated by
the grandson of Mr. Silver, Robert Hanson.

The business development as indicated by the statements of assets of the local banks show that on June 1,
1913, the First National Bank of Ronan had assets totaling $35,396 84, and the Ronan State Bank had assets
of $93,253.61 One bank serves Ronan today — The Ronan
State Bank — which has assets of $3,756,785.36. H. E.
Olsson is the president and general manager.

The city government of Ronan was first organized in 1912, with E. H. Rathbone elected to serve as the first mayor. Harry Holland is presently serving as mayor of the Center City.

According to the 1960 census, the population of Ronan was 1334.

— St. Ignatius —

St. Ignatius is by far the oldest town on the reservation, having been founded in 1854 by the Jesuit Fathers who established the St. Ignatius Mission. Before the founding of the Mission, it was known as The Rendezvous — a gathering place for the Indians.

The settlement began to expand in 1871, when Alexander Demers migrated from Canada and located at St. Ignatius, building a general store, hotel, and livery barn. On February 20, 1872, the town was put on the map with the establishment of a post office. Isadore Cohn was appointed the first postmaster. Prior to this time, the mail had been delivered by pony express.

St. Ignatius became a popular trading point. Indians and the white men who had married into tribes did their trading with Demers and their praying with the Fathers of the Mission. And so it went until 1902, when George H. Beckwith established the Beckwith Mercantile Company.

Born, in 1870, at St. Leonard, New Brunswick, Canada, George Beckwith came to Montana in 1886. In 1888, he went to work for Eddy Hammond & Company in Missoula, and later married the sister of C. H. McLeod, president of the Missoula Mercantile Company. With the establishment of the Beckwith Mercantile and grain elevators in St. Ignatius and Ravalli, George Beckwith became a pioneer business man willing to trust his future with that of the reservation.

189

St. Ignatius as it appears today, 1962

(Meiers Studio Photo)

St. Ignatius slowly expanded as other businesses were added — a newspaper, the Mission State Bank, and others. Some survived and some went under, but the town continued to grow. Business fluctuated, and for two decades prior to 1945, St. Ignatius was without a bank. On April 16, 1945, the Lake County Bank opened its doors to depositors, and has since become a power in the area. The organizers of the bank were W. R. Kelly, N. M Stubblefield, Fred Gariepy, Harry Miller, Homer Welch, and Melvin Udall. Presently under the leadership of Fred Gariepy as president, the Lake County Bank has assets over 1¼ million dollars.

In 1938, the town of St. Ignatius was incorporated with George Beckwith serving as the first mayor and P A. Flatten as the first clerk Other mayors who have served the city are C H Papenfuss, Les Nelson, M M. Stubblefield, Homer Welch, Wilfred Dubay, Woodrow Phillips, Elmer Freshour, and J. J Chipman who has served from 1957 to the present time Fred Gariepy has been the city clerk since 1947.

In 1954, St Ignatius held it Centennial Celebration, honoring 100 years since the founding of the Mission. Bishop Spellman of New York City was the principal figure at the elaborate observances.

St. Ignatius was without a newspaper for many years until 1953 when the St. Ignatius Post went into publication with Millard L Bullerdick as publisher Mr Bullerdick retired in 1960, and Ray Loman took over the editorial duties

The newest post office building on the reservation is located in St. Ignatius Jess Simpkins has been the postmaster since October 15, 1940. The U.S. Indian Irrigation Service makes its headquarters in St. Ignatius, and the population of the town, third largest on the reservation, is 940.

Arlee, in southern part of reservation, 1962
(Meiers Studio Photo)

— Arlee —

The community of Arlee had its beginning in the spring of 1856 with the establishment of the Jocko Agency by the government. In 1861, a flour mill and a saw mill were built, and in 1870, the Jocko Trading Post was established about two miles east of the present site of Arlee.

The building of the Northern Pacific Railway in 1882 brought about the establishment of the Arlee post office. The route of the railway through to the west coast missed the small settlement at the Jocko Agency by two miles, so the new post office, named for the Indian Chief, Arlee, was established on April 27, 1882, at the present site of Arlee. Ludger C. Tuott was appointed the first postmaster.

In 1883, the Hammond Mercantile Company of Missoula (later known as the Missoula Mercantile Company) opened a general store in Arlee where the Demers Mercantile now stands. Mr. Combs of Missoula was sent to Arlee to manage the operation, and he made his home in

192

the rear of the store. One summer evening, Combs was awakened by a drunken Indian who wanted more liquor. The Indian threatened to break-in if Combs didn't give him a bottle of whiskey Combs didn't argue with the Indian long — he fired a shot through the window into the darkness, and killed the intruder, as he was forcibly gaining entrance to the store.

Some of the Indians at the agency were riled at the incident and made threats of revenge. Officials at the Jocko Agency came to the aid of Combs, and contacted the Northern Pacific officials who dispatched a helper-engine out of Missoula. Under cover of darkness, the men whisked Combs out of the rear of the store and helped him board the train, which took him to Missoula without incident.

Alex Demers of St. Ignatius lent a helping hand to the managerless store until his brother, Hector Demers, arrived from Montreal, Canada, and assumed control. In 1888, Hector was killed in a railroad switching mishap, and Alec Dow became the manager. A memorable event took place while Dow had the store Coxsey's Army camped in Arlee for several days and had to be fed. An army travels on its stomach, and thanks to Alec Dow, Coxsey's Army traveled on horse meat and hogs which were furnished by the general store for a price.

Several changes were made in the ownership of the general store until 1900, when Alexander Demers took possession and retained it. In 1908, his son — Louis A. Demers, who had been working for the Missoula Mercantile — joined the firm in Arlee Louis Demers was born at St. Ignatius in 1883, and since that time he has seen a myriad of changes in the reservation country. The life of Arlee, in retrospect, has been the life of Louis A. Demers.

No man has contributed more to the development of the Jocko valley than he.

In 1911, the Demers Mercantile Company was incorporated by Louis and his brother, Lambert, and in 1912, they built the present store building which housed a business that was always at the service of the Jocko valley community

This small community is rich in early day pioneer history Settling and developing this country in the late 1800's were such men as Alexander Morigeau, Alex McLeod, and Chief Arlee The descendants of these pioneers, and others, have all contributed to the betterment of Arlee, and have played a prominent part in the athletic history of the Arlee high school

The town has had several postmasters since 1882, but none has served longer than the present one, Kenneth Le Compte, who cancelled his first stamp in 1936. According to the 1960 census, the population of Arlee was two hundred people.

— Ravalli —

The exact circumstances surrounding the naming of the community of Ravalli are not known, but it is assumed that it was named for the popular Jesuit Father, Anthony Ravalli, who was responsible for the building of the new St Mary's Mission Church in the Bitter Root in the 1850's. It is known that the Ravalli post office was established on February 17, 1887, and Charles A. Stillinger was the first postmaster

Ravalli was a beehive of business activity in the early 1890's with the building of the Great Northern Railway through the upper Flathead. Thousands of tons of freight were channeled from the Northern Pacific railhead at Ravalli to Polson and thence across the lake to Somers and Kalispell From 1908 until 1910, with the

194

Ravalli, junction of US Highways 10 and 93

shipment of the Pablo buffalo herd to Canada and the arrival of optimistic homesteaders, there wasn't a busier place on the reservation. The town consisted of Frank Worden's General Store and post office, the NP railway agency, Tom Ethell's Buffalo Park Hotel, The Bateman Hotel and Livery Barns, the Beckwith Grain Elevators, and other smaller businesses, plus the school house which was also used as a public meeting place. The town was alive with emigrants and stage lines and the ensuing activity created by both.

Today the community of Ravalli is a peaceful place. The main activity is the operation of the State Highway Department maintenance personnel who are located in Ravalli. Robert S. Marshal is the supervisor in charge and he is assisted by B. F. Black. Proprietors of the general store are Mr. and Mrs. E. L. Rowley, and Mrs. Rowley is also the postmaster.

— Dixon —

The first historic record of the community of Dixon occurred in 1812, when David Thompson and his party were camped near the area. On March 1st of that year the group was guided through the reservation to see the Flathead Lake and the Mission Mountains.

Nearly a century elapsed before there was need of a post office however On April 18, 1904, the Dixon post office was established, and Charles E. Shelledy was appointed the first postmaster. It is presumed that the town was named for Governor Joseph M. Dixon.

The town put on a burst of growth around 1909. Some of the prominent businesses included the H. F. Daniels General Merchandise Store, the H. C. Neffner Lumber Yard, the Ben Raymond Livery Barn, and the Madsen Hotel. Pioneer businessmen included Don McDonald, Tom Cantrell and Frank Bowles. John Morkert was the Northern Pacific Railway section foreman, and Lee T Butcher was the clerk at the depot. The Farmer's and Merchant's Bank took care of the deposits and withdrawals. The main spoke in the wheel was L. H. Jeannott, who operated a general store from 1911 until 1946.

The hopes and dreams of the town were based on transportation. Any ideas the city fathers had in regard to becoming a river port were soon dispelled when the river boat, The City of Dixon, met its match in the rapids of the river, and was later destroyed by fire. For many years, the community was quite active as a railhead, not only with the arrival of homesteaders, but later, in 1917, when the Northern Pacific built the Dixon-Polson line. But now this too is gone, and Dixon has settled comfortably into the role of serving the local people.

Dixon, Montana, 1962

(Meiers Studio Photo)

The Flathead Indian Agency is located in the area. Albert Paul is the proprietor of the pioneer Jeannott Store. In addition to the store, the town consists of a restaurant, service station and garage, a tavern and two churches. Edith G. Daniels is the postmaster.

— Perma —

The community of Perma is wrapped up in the life of one person. Edward C. Mulick was born in Perma in 1911, and continues to make his home and business there. Mr. Mulick has a general store, cafe, and tavern, and he has been the postmaster since 1942. His wife assists him in the overall operation of the town's business. During the harvest months of August, September, and October, Al W. Olson operates the grain elevator which is located in the community.

Perma, located on Flathead river, on reservation

At one time, the area was served by a two-room school and a railroad depot. The school house and depot are still there, but are no longer occupied.

— Camas Prairie —

Camas Prairie, just over the hill from Perma, has seen better days. There used to be a general store and a two-room school house in active operation, but today the store stands abandoned. The school house is far from abandoned, but has two capable teachers and a well-equipped school bus. The chairman of the board of education is pioneer, Archie Knerr, who lived on the reservation long before the area was opened for homesteading.

— Lone Pine —

Since the early days of the homesteaders, Freeman H. Halverson has been the main merchant of Lone Pine with his general store, implement house, and garage. Mr.

198

Halverson was also the postmaster. In 1947, he sold his business interests to Frank Herzig, but retained the post office duties until 1951 when Mr. Herzig was appointed postmaster.

Another veteran pioneer of the area is Prof. John McCoy, who was the Superintendent of the Lone Pine Public School system for many years until his recent retirement.

The lone pine from which the town took its name, is located one-fourth mile east and one-half mile south of the present site of the community. Originally the town was at the site of the lone pine, but the buildings — and the town — were moved, and the tree remained.

— Niarada —

. Niarada was the main trading place of the early-day stockmen who lived in the area — men such as Angus McDonald, Johnny Herman, and Max Matt In 1913, Mary E Borden, grandmother of Amelia Gipe of Valley View, was the proprietor of the general store and the postmaster She carried these duties until 1923 when Fred Hughes acquired them In 1927, Mr. and Mrs Allen Voorhies purchased the business, and served the community until 1961 when they sold out to Mrs Patsy Wood. Since that time, Mrs Wood has been the postmaster and proprietor of the store Nearby is the Community Hall where dances, socials, and community gatherings are held

— Pablo —

The town of Pablo, named for Michel Pablo, is the youngest town on the reservation When the Northern Pacific spur line from Dixon to Polson was nearing completion, the U S government held a public lot sale of the townsite on September 13, 1917 By the time the track was

Pablo, new mills have helped its economy
(Meiers Studio Photo)

being laid through the area in October, buildings — both business and residential — were being erected and the town of Pablo was showing signs of coming to life.

The first postmaster of Pablo was Bert Dimmick, and subsequent postmasters have been Fred L. Stimson and Elsie Garbe.

The businessmen of the new town were energetic and enthusiastic, and many of them openly predicted that Pablo would soon be larger than Ronan and Polson. Some of the businesses were: L. C. Burner's Blacksmith Shop, the Palace Hotel, Hotel de Pablo, The Pablo Press, the Farmer's State Bank, O. G. Olson & Carl Iverson, Doering & Durand, Dr. Squire, dentist; Gump Law Offices, Dr. Powell, M.D.; Walker's Barber Shop, Carlyle's Grocery, Shennum & McIntyre, Bates Theater, E. O. Shreve Insurance, Saxton Machine Shop, Maynard Lumber Company, the Estes Dance Hall, and many others. E. R. Rowan was the first depot agent.

200

Many businesses folded during the 1920's, and the small town sagged, but the establishment of a cheese factory by Lawrence Otter revived activities to a certain extent. Automobile travel and good roads soon took their toll in favor of the larger towns, and Pablo ceased to grow.

In 1957 and 1958, the economy of the community was given a major boost with the establishment of sawmills and a door and sash factory in the area. A new subdivision is being opened up, and the future is again looking brighter for this reservation town.

— Post Creek —

When Bert Dimmick left Pablo in 1927, he and Mrs. Dimmick moved south to Post Creek and established a store near the Post Creek Pavilion on the old state road. When the highway was changed, the store made the change too, and moved to the present site. At the present time, the store is being operated by E. D. Cordis.

— Moiese —

When homesteaders settled the Moiese valley in 1910, they built two school houses — one to the south of the valley, and one to the north. They also erected a community hall. With the valley becoming well-populated with settlers, and the establishment of the bison range nearby, there was need for a general store and post office. Fulfilling the need, the people of the community got together and built a store in one day. On May 4, 1918, James D Sloan became the first postmaster of Moiese and the proprietor of the new general store. Since that time, the postmaster-proprietors have been E. R. Rowan, William Kinney, John Wall, E. J. Wamsley, 1934-1959, and Mrs Lucille Marsh.

— Charlo —

The townsite of Tabor was named in honor of a reclamation engineer, E. F. Tabor, in the early 1900's, but when the post office was established on February 26, 1918, it was named for the famous Indian Chief Charlo inasmuch as many of his descendants were allotted acreage in this area. The first postmaster was Pontus G. Haegg.

In the heart of good farming country, Charlo grew fast. Some of the pioneer businesses included the Erwin Wilson Lumber Company, Frank Carrington, contractor; E. W. McMenus Pool Hall; R. D. Watson Feed Store; The First National Bank with A. A. Lesseg, cashier; Bill McDonald's Dance Hall; The Charlo Star with J. C. Schleppegrell, publisher; Kaiser and Harrah, honey men; Mr. and Mrs. H. A. Hatfield, who ran a cafe and bakery; and the reliable G. W. Wamsley Mercantile Company. The Mercantile, which opened in 1917, is now under the management of Francis Wamsley, son of the founders. Other pioneers still in business are the Wiebke Brothers, who run a general store; Jack Wilson has a service station and garage; "Tiny" Brown operates a hotel and tavern, and there is the Charlo Paint and Glass Company and the Evans Lumber Company.

The people of the Charlo area are co-operative minded. In 1927 and 1928, a co-operative creamery and cheese factory was established, as well as an up-to-date freezer unit. In addition, an oil department with a service station dealing at wholesale and retail levels was founded with the Wiebke brothers as managers.

On September 6, 1938, farmers of Round Butte, Ronan, St. Ignatius, Moiese, and Charlo organized the Western Montana Co-op Seed Growers Association. The membership reached approximately 400, and the association is still doing business in Charlo.

Charlo, the "Co-op Town"
(Meiers Studio Photo)

Shortly thereafter, the progressive citizens negotiated a long-term lease on a well belonging to Consolidated Dairies, and now own their own water system. Charlo also has a sewage system and an efficient volunteer fire department. Postmasters who have served the community include Lee Biggerstaff, 1934-1959; Dorothy Adamson, 1959-1961; and Lawrence Driscoll, 1961 to the present time. The population of Charlo, according to the 1960 census, was 200.

— Round Butte —

From 1910 until 1912, the farming community just west of Ronan was called Horte, named for a homesteader who operated a country store. Two miles down the road was the Round Butte Mercantile Company, operated by Lars Beck. The post office was located in the Round Butte Mercantile, so it assumed the name of Round Butte.

203

The community gets its name from a round butte which is located just east of the schools and church.

Today the stores are closed, although an occupant resides in one of them, and the post office is no longer in existence. Round Butte is just the name of a farming community.

— Leon —

From 1910 until 1920, the community of Leon — located between St. Ignatius and Charlo — was on the map of the reservation. It consisted of a general store, a grade school, a high school, and a community clubhouse. But the only reminder of the village today is the community hall which is still used by the people of the area.

— Radio or Seines —

The rural area of Irvine Flats was served by a trading post which carried the name of Radio, possibly due to the fact that one family had a radio. (This has not been verified however.) The name was later changed to Seines, in honor of John Seines who was a popular homesteader of the area. There were four school houses in the community, and a settler on every homestead unit in the valley. John David Lyons, the father of Kenneth Lyons of Polson, was the first postmaster. Today there are no reminders of the early days, other than memories.

— Finley Point —

At the entrance to Finley Point is a modern-day trading post. The Finley Point Store, which is currently operated by Mr. and Mrs. Joe Stevens. Originally built by L. E. Brooks, the store was sold to Gwynne "Porky" Neifert, and later was operated by Elmer Ingraham. Across from the store is a popular meeting place for the people of the Finley Point area, the Montecahto Clubhouse.

— Big Arm —

The townsite of Big Arm taking its name from the big arm of the Flathead Lake, came into existence with a rush after Polson and some of the other reservation towns were established. A lot sale was held by the government, and most of the lots sold for a good price.

The site officially became a town with the establishment of a post office on February 27, 1911. Miss Marian F. Lamb, who operated a general store with her father and younger sister, Hazel, was appointed the first postmaster. Other business people included C. L. Sterling, blacksmith; Tip Goff and A. C. Betz, grocers; Bill Paine, barber; J. O. Rude and sons, general merchandise; John McGrann, clerical work and notary; and the Brammer Livery Barn. The town also boasted a lumber yard, restaurant, hotel, pool hall, a newspaper — The Big Arm Graphic, a boat warehouse and agent for the navigation companies, a Catholic Church, a Protestant Church, a two-room schoolhouse and a dance hall. One thing was overlooked in the early days of Big Arm — someone forgot to start a bank.

The businessmen, like the homesteaders in the community, were full of vim and vigor, and many dreams were made only to be broken. Farmers found their homesteads would not sustain them, and many moved away. And so it was with many of the businesses. O. A. Knox bought out the Rude Mercantile Company, and soon fell heir to about everything that was left of the business section. As time went on, this business also faltered, and only the school and a few residences remained.

In 1936, Mr. and Mrs Harry Ross located in Big Arm, built a store and five tourist cabins, and constructed a dock. They brought in a supply of fishing boats, and soon

Big Arm, where fishing is always good!

were in the tourist business. In 1949, they sold the business to Minnie and George Davis. Mrs. Davis was appointed postmaster, and George Davis became a Lake County commissioner. The Rosses enlarged the tourist facilities, and accommodations were improved with the building of Mary and Peg's Restaurant. Big Arm today is a quiet place by the side of the lake, making the most of its potential.

— Elmo —

Elmo officially began to function on April 10, 1911, when Aaron A. Stuckman was appointed postmaster of the newly established post office. Andrew Wilhelm, who operated a general store not far from the present site of Elmo, succeeded Mr. Stuckman as postmaster. Years later, the store and post office were moved to the present site

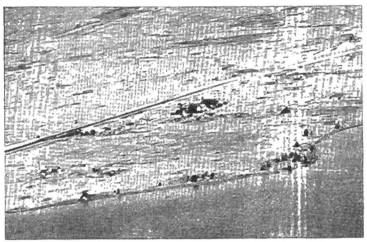

Elmo, historic camp of early-day Kootenais
(Meiers Studio Photo)

and functioned in the home now occupied by the Lester Maas family. Earlier, in 1912, the building had been used as a restaurant and hotel. There was also a store and livery barn managed by Jake Knerr and Louis Frye, who succeeded Wilhelm as postmaster.

In 1926, George and Anna Crouch bought the store and Mrs. Crouch became the postmaster. In the early thirties, the store building was moved around the block to face the newly-constructed highway. Mrs. Crouch was the proprietor of the store and the postmaster until 1944. The Crouch store is now being operated by Orville Swisher. To the north, two blocks away, is the only other business in Elmo — a store managed by Charlotte Wilhelm who is also the present poastmaster.

The community of Elmo was named for an Indian, David Elmo (Elmier). The log house in which he lived is still standing. Alec Couture, an Indian policeman who keeps law and order among the natives, makes his home near Elmo.

207

— Dayton —

When Uncle Sam established a post office at Dayton on November 6, 1893, and appointed Clarence E. Proctor the first postmaster, the site was just off the reservation limits. Soon after this, Jake Knerr and Charles Frost bought the store from Proctor, and Charles became the postmaster. Frost and Knerr asked for a permit to move the store and post office a few feet to the southeast, and they received permission to do so. When they got the building on wheels, they moved it over two miles to the present site of Dayton, which is inside the reservation boundaries.

Dayton was on the map during the '90's when the Allard Stage Line went through, carrying mail, passengers, and express from Ravalli to Kalispell. Later there was a passenger and mail stage which ran from Dayton to the Hot Springs area.

Dayton, gateway to Lake Mary Ronan resort area
(Meiers Studio Photo)

From 1908 to 1910, the town began to pick up. Harris and Company of Kalispell established a bank which was later taken over by F. A Hacker and H. F. Dwelle, and named the Dayton State Bank. Vinson and Meuli operated livery barns; Copeland's Dayton Leader was published until July of 1917; Riggins had a photo gallery, and he was assisted by the famed Herman Schnitzmeyer, who was homesteading on Wild Horse Island. Oscar Johnson, now of Polson, erected a building which housed a pool hall, barber shop, dance hall, and apartments. There were two general merchandise stores, two hotels, and two restaurants. M. T. Burns became the postmaster and managed the general store.

The water front was alive with activity as grain, livestock, and freight moved in and out of the docks on the steamers. Then the dry years of the twenties and thirties hit, and took their toll in Dayton. The town had more than its share of bad fires, and where there had once been a thriving business, there remained ashes. Not even concrete foundations could give evidence of a building being in existence at one time; when many of the buildings had been constructed in the general rush to get into business quick, they were not placed on solid foundations.

Business picked up during the next decade when the lumber industry started logging operations in the area. Logs from the Great Northern timber stand near Lake Ronan were brought down by rail and dumped into the lake from the cars on the water front.

Today there is no mad rush or wild activity. Old-timers, such as Ewald Heubner who operated the last butcher store in town, and Frankie Proud, an early-day school teacher and secretary-treasurer of the REA in

1948, still make their homes in Dayton and enjoy the quiet life. Roy Commers looks after the timber interests of the Great Northern Railway. Graydon Williams, a native son, is the current postmaster and proprietor of the general store. Other businesses include the Clyde Paro store, the Native Sporting Goods Company, and Liddell's Tavern.

— Camas —

Located in the Little Bitter Root Valley, the townsite of Camas was named by the U. S. government for the medicine root of the Camas plant which was used by the Indians for medicinal purposes. This plant was quite prominent in the Camas valley.

The community of Camas was the home base of five prominent men of the reservation — Swift Courville, Wilkes Markle, T. G. Garcon Demers, Ed Lamoreaux, and Joe Morigeau. From 1909 until 1912, the pioneer businesses included the general merchandise store operated by Fred Pesso and Phil Zeh; Frank Hammons & Son Department Store; Louie Beauregard, blacksmith; Riser's Restaurant; the Camas State Bank; Drs. Crutcher and Henderlite, Mansfield's Grocery Store, and Alex Rhone's newspaper, The Camas Exchange. One of the most outstanding citizens of Camas is Edna Gannaway, a homesteader and early-day school teacher.

B. A. Moore bought the newspaper from Alex Rhone and move it to Hot Springs But Edna Gannaway, a dyed-in-the-wool Camasite, bought the paper from Moore and promptly moved it back to Camas. She named it The Camas Hot Springs Exchange, and for many years the weekly paper extolled the virtues of the Camas-Hot Springs area. Mrs. Gannaway retired in 1959, when the paper was published for the last time.

210

Many people came and went from Camas, but the majority of them went — moving to nearby Hot Springs. Today there is one business remaining in Camas . . . a garage and machine shop operated by Glen Davis.

— Hot Springs —

According to the Post Office Department in Washington, D.C., a post office was established in the Hot Springs area on July 5, 1902, with Frank T. Shields the first postmaster. Authoritative records show that the townsite of Pineville, an eighty acre allotment of T. G. Demers, was platted into lots and put on the market in 1910. Prior to this, the site consisted of two residences, two livery barns, and the Demers Hotel. In the Maillet Addition at this time were the Maillet Hotel and the livery barn which housed the horses used on the stage runs from Plains to Dayton. The Mailett sons, Ed, George, and Louis are currently businessmen of Hot Springs.

In 1912-13, Mr. Ekblad and H. E Smith opened a general store, and Smith was appointed postmaster. At this time the name of the town was changed from Pineville to Hot Springs, and the town began to grow. The reputation of the "mud hole" — the hot mineral springs — began to grow as well and people traveled many miles just to soak their feet in the mud that soothed and healed.

More business houses were erected. Andrew Beckwith became the manager of the M. M. Company. The Camas State Bank moved to Hot Springs. Emedee Jette had the first garage in town, then Holt & Hurst opened one. Carter Bros. featured the latest silent movies, and when H. E. Smith built Nyah Hall, he made installations that enabled the showing of "talkies."

Lamoreaux Addition was platted and added to the town, and one of the first buildings to go up was the

Hot Springs, internationally famous health spa

(Meiers Studio Photo)

Towanda Hotel, which was built in 1917 by James and Margaret Crowley. Furnishing the lumber for the growing community was the Marquardt Brothers' Sawmill, and later the Pitts Sawmill

Deadly fires took their toll in this town, as it did in others on the reservation, but resolute businessmen rebuilt. However, when the bank building was destroyed by fire in 1916, it was not replaced, and there hasn't been a bank in Hot Springs since that time.

The man who gave the biggest boost to the town of Hot Springs was Fred Symes. In 1926, he built what was to become the famous Symes Hotel which featured the mineral baths right in the hotel. The mineral water, known by the early-day Indians as Big Medicine, was later known by thousands of people from all parts of the United States who visited the famous spa. The Symes Hotel is currently managed by Mrs. Del Ducco.

The Flathead Tribal Council for the Confederated Tribes got into the swim when they covered the "mud hole," constructed a swimming pool, and built a new bathhouse. This health resort, which is open the year around, is one of the most popular in the west Tommy Pablo, great-grandson of Michel Pablo, is the manager.

The town of Hot Springs officially began to function as a municipality in February, 1929 Dr. Henderlite was the first regulary elected mayor of the city. Following him in succession were Joe Beebe, 1930-1941; Francis Dalstrom, 1941-1943; Joe Cobeen, 1943-1947; I R. Strange, 1947-1949, Jim Lowney, 1949-1953; Myrtle Demers Myler, 1953-1955; Jim Lowney, 1955-1961; and Delbert Mullen, 1961 to the present time Nellie Hood has been the city clerk since May, 1929. The present postmaster of Hot Springs is Pauline Russell

213

Hot Springs owns its own water system, and, like other towns on the reservation, has low-cost electric rates. The population of the town is 585 inhabitants.

CHAPTER TWENTY
Golden Jubilee — 1910-1960

The golden jubilee celebrations by the different communities on the Reservation marked 50 years of development since the opening of the Reservation in 1910. These events brought out the finest of cooperative spirit among the area residents

Assisting and cooperating with the celebrations, the Reservation Pioneers, through the graciousness of Mrs. George Hepburn, procured the 1909 Allard stagecoach that had run from Ravalli to Polson and return. The coach gave great impetus to the different events and was first entered in the Homestead Days parade at Hot Springs, June 12, 1960. The stagecoach, drawn by six horses with George Piedalue at the helm took first place in its division.

Next Golden Jubilee event was the Man vs. Horse race from Missoula to Polson Contestants in this event were Montana University track star Bill Anderson, Jr. and a Palomino horse owned by Ed Crawford and ridden alternately by Don Olsson and N B. (Slim) Coppedge.

The event attracted statewide interest as the horse won the race in the time of 12 hours and 18 minutes. Anderson retired from the contest after a leg cramp seizure struck him as he loped up Evaro Hill Before retiring, though, he almost reached Ravalli, a distance of nearly 35 miles from the starting line

Next observance was the picnic and barbecue at Moiese on June 25 where the president of the Pioneers was one of the speakers.

A float with Adeline Allard, Pioneer Queen, and her six princesses — Bertha Markle Dolson, Inez Murphy Rollins, Thelma Johnson Herman, Velma Johns Atkinson,

Reservation Pioneers whoop it up during Golden Jubilee celebration at Polson, 1960. Driving the old Allard stage is George Piedalue (Meiers Studio Photo)

Dorothy McGeorge Adamson and Helen Finley Stevens — was entered in the parade at Ronan as was the six-horse stagecoach. Both entries were well received and added much to the July 31 event.

On August 1 the stagecoach completed the run to Missoula with the Bob Schall and George Piedalue horses making the run. Piedalue appeared in the mammoth Missoula centennial parade with the six horses and historic stagecoach. The entry took first place in the horse-drawn vehicle division.

The climax of the Golden Jubilee events came on Aug 20 and 21 with the Golden Jubilee parade at Polson and the reunion and picnic of the Reservation Pioneers at the Polson country club picnic grounds In the parade were the Pioneers' royal party of the queen and princesses riding on a special Pioneer float while George Piedalue took the reins of the six-horse stagecoach and drove that down Main Street.

At the picnic on Sunday, Aug. 21, the event was highlighted by the appearance of the Flathead Fleet, led by the MS Flathead with the Medicine Hat Scottish Bagpipe Band and the Reservation Pioneers royal party aboard All the festivities plus a very large crowd on hand made the golden jubilee picnic a memorable event.

All in all, the Golden Jubilee was a very enjoyable summer for the Reservation Pioneers.

In the last 52 years, since the opening of the reservation to white settlement, the Pioneers have seen a vast change from the horse and buggy days to man traveling faster than sound . . . with a man orbiting the earth in less time than it would take for a man to go from Polson to Ronan in 1910!

How the next 52 years can bring a greater change is difficult for us Pioneers to visualize. But here are best wishes for peace, health and happiness to all, and to all good luck, and may God bless you. We hope that you have liked our book, "The Fabulous Flathead."

The Reservation Pioneers,
J. F. McAlear, President
D. A. Dellwo, Vice-president
Ruth Herreid, Secretary
Gladys Irish, Treasurer
Helen Finley Stevens
J. S. Dillon
Frankie J. Proud
George Piedalue
Ben Williamson, Directors

Reservation Pioneer Directors
Seated from left — Helen Finley Stevens, Frankie J. Proud, Ruth Herreid, Gladys Irish. Standing, from left, J. S. Dillon, George Piedalue, Ben Williamson, D. A. Dellwo, J. F. McAlear

218   (Meiers Studio Photo)

HONOR ROLL
Original Allottees — 1908

Joseph Allard
Adaline Allard
Eva Mae Allard
Joe Antiste
Mary Stasso Antiste
Gladys Allard Bentley
Joseph Bisson
Alexander Clairmont
Matilda Jette Connerley
Ernest Clairmont
Olive J Clairmont
Alexander Couture
Willie A Dupuis
Elizabeth Minesinger Dupuis
Willard R. Dupuis
Robert Dupuis Sr
Angela Matt Houseman
Flora McDonald Felsman
George Jette
Amedee Jette

Matilda McDonald Irwin
James Kalowatt
Cecille Stasso Kalowatt
Rosalie P Matt
Archie McDonald
Sophie Dumont McDonald
Johnny McDonald
Charles Minesinger
Fred Miles
Jesse Miles
Norville (Kie) Morais
Antoine Pariseau
Napoleon Plouffe, Jr
Theodore Plouffe
Collette Matt Plouffe
Nellie Miles Piper
Oliva Jette Pronovost
Vera Dupuis Voorhies
Helen Finley Stevens
Margaret McDonald Trickey

Homesteaders

A L Atkinson Round Butte	1911	Geo A Freshour St Ignatius	1917
Harry L Andrews Hot Springs	1914	Carey H Gordon Ronan	1910
Lee Biggerstaff Charlo	1912	A W Goranson Round Butte	1910
Martin O Bjorge Garcon Gulch	1910	H M Hendrickson Moiese	1915
Golden Bibee Big Arm	1911	George Halverson Irvine Flats	1910
A T Baumgartner Polson	1910	Alfred M Hanson Lone Pine	1911
Joe W Cernik Ronan	1910	Eric Jorgensen Perma	1910
D A Dellwo Charlo	1910	B F Johnson, Sr. Round Butte	1910
Mary Cassidy Dellwo Charlo	1915	Bob Johnson Moiese	1910

Florence Haegg Johnson	1910	**Widows of Homesteaders**
Round Butte		
Tollef Hoye	1910	Millicent Alexander, Widow of
Lone Pine		Wm S Alexander 1911
Marius Hoye	1916	Big Draw
Niarada		Maybelle Cook, Widow of
Tom Lavin	1910	Frank A Cook 1910
Hot Springs		Charlo
Henry Bert Lewis	1910	Mary Christensen, Widow of
Arlee		N A Christensen 1910
J W Leverich	1910	Polson
Round Butte		Mary English, Widow of
Richard D Lowe	1910	Frank English 1910
Polson		Charlo
Elsie Jahnke Marquardt	1912	Thora N French, Widow of
Niarada		Lee D French 1910
F M Murdick	1910	Polson
Valley View		Isobel R. Goble, Widow of
W G Mountjoy	1915	H H Goble 1910
Lone Pine		St Ignatius
J F McAlear	1917	Elizabeth Harlan, Widow of
Valley View		Fred Harlan 1910
Helen Haegg Needham	1914	Polson
Round Butte		Dora Forman, Widow of
Jos G Piedalue	1911	Wm H Forman 1910
Charlo		Polson
Gjert Reksten	1911	Clara Peschel, Widow of
Irvine Flats		Bruno Peschel 1910
Margaret Dwyer Roberts	1914	Ronan
Charlo		Frankie J Proud, Widow of
M E Schoonover	1910	Roy E Proud 1911
Moiese		Dayton
F P Sampson	1911	Bell Reynolds, Widow of
Hot Springs		C E Reynolds 1910
John Seines	1910	Polson
Irvine Flats		Laura Siphers, Widow of
J M Smith	1910	John W Siphers 1910
Irvine Flats		Arlee
James S Smith	1911	Millie Ratcliff, Widow of
Irvine Flats		F J Ratcliff 1910
L O Smith	1912	Lone Pine
Moiese		Lettie Sandage, Widow of
Walter A Standley	1912	Otis Sandage 1914
Hot Springs		Polson
H E Smith	1913	Amy Sallee, Widow of
Hot Springs		Samuel S Sallee 1911
Ralph R Tower	1910	Hot Springs
Polson		Mrs Ray Turnquist, Widow of
Ben Williamson	1911	Ray Turnquist 1910
St Ignatius		Round Butte

Members of the Reservation Pioneers

A. L Atkinson
Velma J Atkinson
Joseph Allard
Adeline Allard
Gene P Allard
Dorothy V Allard
Millicent Alexander
Billie Broyles
Marie Sallee Byrns
Morris C Bjorge
Martin O Bjorge
Mrs Martin O Bjorge
Lee Biggerstaff
Helen Bratton
Alice Sheen Crawford
Clarence A Brown
Lottie Barnekoff
Mabel Sallee Coon
N B Coppedge
Ruth I Coppedge
John S Coleman
Walter L Conway
Thorna Brown Conway
Ray J Cary
Beulah Caffrey
Ilma Carney
J S Dillon
D A Dellwo
Mrs D A Dellwo
R R Davis
Willard R Dupuis
Lawrence Driscoll
Wilfred Dubay
Bert Dolson
Bertha Markle Dolson
Fred Eckley — Anna Eckley
Bernice Elkins
Geo A Freshour
Zulema Freshour
Thora N French
Lillian M Flanagan
Earl S Ferrell
Mabel Douglas Frolin
Max Garbe

C E Goettsche
Maxine Gilbert
Ethel Mayer Harley
Alfred Hilton
Ruth Herreid
James C Howser
Klonda Howser
Thelma A Herman
Inez Hanson
Marius Hoye
Ottis Harrison
Eva Howard
Robert J Hamel
Elizabeth Harlan
Alpha Omega Sallee Hedin
Nick Herak
Viola Herak
Dora Harmon
A M Hanson
Mrs A M Hanson
Elmer R Hagel
Gladys Irish

Robert T Johnson
Arle O Johnson
Bessie M Johnson
Mrs J A Johnson
Ernest A Johnson
William Keller, Sr
Maud Kerns
Ruth Kerns
Helen Oktabec Linderman
Robert S Marshall
Fred Miles
Cora King Marquardt
Dorothy McKnight
J F McAlear
Leonard Newgard
Margaret L Oie
Joseph G Piedalue
George Piedalue
Ruby Piedalue
Peder Pedersen
Frankie J Proud
Bill Pickett

221

Inez Rollins
John A Rhone
Edna Sallee Reifschneider
Margaret Dwyer Roberts
Millie Ratcliff
Amy A Sallee
Stephen Samuel Sallee
Milton E Schoonover
Leland Schoonover
Marie Streible
Helen Stevens
Bertha Sorensen
J M Smith
John Seines
Nora C Smock
Hazel Strodtbeck
Gladys Seines
J P Seines
H E Smith
Lillis O Smith
Minnie M Seiller
Walter A Standley

Myrtle I Sterling
C L Sterling
Grace Sterling
Alice Sinclair
John Sizemore
Bob Spencer
Ruth Spencer
Leon Thomas
Boyd Thompson
Alma Thompson
Ralph R Tower
Flora Ventley
Walter von Euen
Ted Vander Ende
Wm W Von Segen
Daisy Warner
Ben Williamson
Mrs Ben Williamson
Mary Wright
Emma Wynne
L G Wymore

Printed in the USA
CPSIA information can be obtained
at www.ICGtesting.com
LVHW041329011123
762550LV00013B/1